A Letter from Chuck

When we walk in Jesus's footsteps, we can't help but notice the devoted, faith-filled women who followed Him. All were impacted and changed by Him. The centuries between our cultures have softened the scenes for us, but to the people of His day, *Jesus's invitations and responses were nothing less than shocking*.

To us, the picture of Jesus talking with a woman doesn't seem so strange. But the culture at the turn of the first century put women just a notch above animals. A woman was considered property—first of her father, then of her husband, and then of her son when she was widowed. Back then, a woman's opinion didn't matter. The majority thought *she* didn't matter. A woman had little hope of survival apart from a man.

Women barely survived near the bottom of the social ladder. They were thought responsible for much of the evil in the world. If a woman spoke in public to a man who was not her husband, it was assumed she was having an illicit relationship with him, making it grounds for divorce . . . or worse. Furthermore, a woman was not allowed to eat in the same room with a gathering of men, to be taught Scripture with men, or to enter the inner court of the temple to worship with men. Each morning, if you can believe it, a Pharisee began his day by thanking God that he had not been born a Gentile, a woman, or a slave.

But not so with Jesus.

While even respectable men didn't give women the time of day, Jesus went out of His way to speak with them . . . in broad daylight. It would have been a topic for the tabloids! He welcomed women to His side. *Scandalous!* He was supportive, considerate, and caring of women—especially the ones who most needed help. He broke through oppressive, ugly cultural rules and rescued women from painful pasts, demonic control, and crippling diseases.

Jesus also willingly went against the grain of acceptable religious practices. Instead of limiting His teaching to the "men-only" part of the synagogue, Jesus also taught in places where women could have front row seats—on hillsides, in the marketplace, beside a well, and in the women's area of the temple. He used illustrations women could readily relate to—a lost coin, yeast rising in bread, a persistent knocking on a neighbor's door at midnight.

Not only did Jesus notice women, He called them out of the shadows and into faith. It wasn't by accident that many of His recorded conversations were with women or that many of His miracles placed women in starring roles. Jesus deliberately chose it to be this way. What's more, women were among His best students and most dynamic and daring disciples. No wonder women loved His instruction! I think the way women responded to Him made Jesus smile. He saw their faith. And His example of grace, mercy, and compassion was no less than a seismic shift to everyone on the scene! Spiritually speaking, Jesus made no distinction between men and women. He simply related to people on the basis of their faith in God—or lack thereof.

You know what I find surprising? The consistency of Scripture's description of the women who followed Jesus! They were faithful, sacrificial, and serving. Were the women perfect? Of course not. Did they follow Jesus perfectly? No, no one does.

But they stood close enough to Jesus to catch the look in His eyes. His grace captured them! Just so they could be part of what Jesus was doing, many women were content with an anonymous role on His ministry team. Serving however it was needed, giving financial support out of their own means, sitting at His feet, worshiping Him, feeding Him and His men, and eventually caring for His broken, crucified body. These were brave women—committed women—who linked their arms with His for the proclamation of something bigger. Something more wonderful than the world had ever known.

Jesus said of one such faithful woman, "Truly I say to you, wherever this gospel is preached in the whole world, what this woman has done will also be spoken of in memory of her" (Matthew 26:13).

On the pages of this magazine, I invite you to spend some time getting to know the ladies whose lives intersected with Jesus's. They were there at the moment of His arrival, in and out of the towns He visited, at His cross and His tomb, and by His side at amazing ministry moments. Like you and me, each tells a different story of how His life impacted hers. Together they give us living, breathing examples of the power of God to change lives. Some had to clean up. Some had to step up. He called others to speak up . . . or walk up . . . or simply show up. Just as He does with us today, He invited them to reflect His life to their generation.

As you encounter these women whose lives Jesus touched, I hope you will see your own story woven through theirs and experience your life in Christ as never before.

Alongside you in this great journey of faith,

Chuck Swindoll

Charles R. Swindoll

Inside This Issue

WOMEN IN THE LIFE OF JESUS

> The divine perspective says, "Lord, I'm facing a crisis. But I know I can trust You; I want to trust You. Lord, I submit. I resign myself to Your plan. And with great delight, I wait upon Your answer."
>
> —Chuck Swindoll

WHAT KIND OF WAITER ARE YOU? 31

As you slip out of bed each morning, thank God for His love and His calm, fresh reminders that this new day is under His control. Quietly state the encouraging truth: God loves me.

—Chuck Swindoll

FEATURES

Life's Detours

A Look in the Mirror

Relate Better

You and God

LIGHTWEIGHT

Ask Yourself

Be Inspired

Live Well

Every Woman

Insight For Living Brings You . . .

> *"When the sound of your greeting reached my ears, the baby leaped in my womb for joy. And blessed is she who believed that there would be a fulfillment of what had been spoken to her by the Lord."*
>
> —*Luke 1:44–45*

Fellowship

Sharing in the Mystery

Elizabeth had no clue what could be keeping her husband.

Those who stood beside her outside the temple wondered the same. His priestly duties were routine—Zacharias had been chosen by lot to burn incense before the Lord—so the delay in coming back out gave cause for concern.

Finally, Zacharias emerged—and frantically approached Elizabeth. The elderly priest could not speak but kept pointing to his throat, then to the temple, then to the sky, motioning with his hands. *What was wrong?* Elizabeth furrowed her brow, watching him. Finally, she understood: he had seen a vision in the temple. *But of what—and why?*

After Elizabeth calmed him down, Zacharias took his wife's wrinkled hands in his own, placing both on her abdomen. She searched his eyes for an explanation . . . and saw there a glimmer. She jerked her hands from her barren womb to her mouth, "Do you mean, we . . . ?"

Zacharias flashed a wide, toothy grin . . . and winked at her.

In the course of time, Elizabeth became pregnant. She could not contain her joy! "This is the way the Lord has dealt with me in the days when He looked with favor upon me, to take away my disgrace among men" (Luke 1:25). Her husband was mute throughout her pregnancy—a discipline for not believing the vision at first. But he was still able to scribble down what the vision had revealed: Elizabeth would bear the forerunner of the Messiah!

Six months passed; Elizabeth could feel movement and flutterings, the delightful presence of the precious infant in her womb. But when Elizabeth's young relative Mary came to visit, Elizabeth felt something different. "When Elizabeth heard Mary's greeting, the baby leaped in her womb; and Elizabeth was filled with the Holy Spirit" (1:41). No doubt the Spirit of God communicated to her, in effect, "Mary's carrying a child, the Messiah!" (See Luke 1:42–45.)

Although Elizabeth was stunned, surprised, and certainly curious about how God had brought it all about, she never hesitated in believing God. Why would she have? She was carrying a miracle in her own womb. She had already learned that God specializes in impossibilities.

After five months alone in a house with a mute husband, what a delight it must have been for Elizabeth to share with Mary the details of her pregnancy.

And what a relief it must have been for Mary, not only to be with someone who believed her story but to learn from her cousin's experience! She spent the next three months soaking up Elizabeth's wisdom on everything from home remedies to spiritual strength. Mary would need it all that lonely night in a Bethlehem stable. And God knew it. He knew all the deep needs of these women, and He chose to fill those needs through relationship with each other.

—*Charles R. Swindoll*

YOU GO, GIRL!

Someone you know today who is *younger* than you could use your help figuring out how to live a godly life. And someone you know today who is *older* than you could help you figure out how to live a godly life. And sometimes age doesn't matter at all!

Wisdom is not attached to a number. And the truth is, you need support and guidance in all stages of life. There's a name for that kind of help: *mentoring*. And throughout Scripture, particularly in Titus 2:3–5, mentoring is described in word and example.

So how can you be a mentor?

1. *Just be yourself*. You might say, "Well, I'm no mentor." No offense here, but you're older than someone, right? Someone can learn from you. If you've been a Christian for a while, you know more about walking with Christ than someone around you just by sheer experience. Start with your own children, if you have them. And then, when they've grown and left the nest, you'll have others that come near. Have one or two young women under your wings for the rest of your life.

2. *Ask questions too*. The pressure isn't on you—it's a relationship. Give and take. For a mentor, the emphasis isn't on teaching but *training*. In the course of doing life together, you will talk and walk with the woman whose life you're influencing. And as you get involved (without meddling!), instead of being depleted by the investment, you'll find it fills you up!

3. *Affirm her faith*. As you observe her life and her choices, praise what you can. Say, "I can see the faith in you. I've gotten to know you, I understand you, I realize how you're put together, and I can see how you're growing in the Lord." Few words give greater encouragement than a heartfelt, "You go, girl. You're on track."

So why would you want to be a mentor?

Because believe it or not, you *need* to pour your life into others. If you don't, all that wisdom and knowledge and savvy that young women are craving from you will stagnate and grow bitter inside you. Eventually, you'll stop growing . . . and you'll waste away. God knew what He was doing when He created women with a need for relationships—now use it for His glory. BP

She's Your Closest Friend, but Is She **IRON**?

As iron sharpens iron,
so one man sharpens another.
(Proverbs 27:17 NIV)

- You're the hostess; your "never-fail" dish is to be on the menu. One problem: nobody likes it. *Does your friend clue you in . . . in time?*
- He's bad for you. Everybody knows it—maybe even you—but their lips are sealed. It's life-changing decision time . . . but first, coffee with your friend. *What does she say?*
- It's 3 a.m. You've just gotten word—you've lost someone. You dial your friend. You rage; you sob. *What do you hear on the other end?*
- You love Jesus. But, lately, you haven't paid Him much mind . . . and it shows. Over lunch with your friend, your shared faith comes up. *What two cents does she offer?*

Now, ask yourself,
Am I IRON?

Every Woman Needs a Girlfriend

When we were young, we had no idea what incredible joys and unexpected sorrows lay ahead. Nor did we know how much we would need each other. Every woman needs a girlfriend.

- Girlfriends bring casseroles and scrub your bathroom when you're sick.
- Girlfriends keep your children and your secrets.
- Girlfriends know the difference between giving you space and keeping their distance.
- Girlfriends feel your pain when you lose a job or a marriage.
- Girlfriends instinctively discern when "don't tell a soul" means "don't tell a soul, I mean it."
- Girlfriends don't keep a calendar that lets them know who hosted last.
- Girlfriends give you someone to care about other than yourself or your family.
- Girlfriends listen when your children break your heart.
- Girlfriends stand beside you at the front of the church—at your wedding or beside a casket.
- Girlfriends weather the seasons of life.

The angel said to her, "Do not be afraid, Mary; for you have found favor with God. And behold, you will conceive in your womb and bear a son, and you shall name Him Jesus. . . ." Mary said to the angel, "How can this be, since I am a virgin?" . . . The angel answered . . . "Nothing will be impossible with God."

—Luke 1:30–31, 34–35, 37

Jesus & Mary of Nazareth

Amazed

Humbly Facing the Impossible

Six months after delivering a startling announcement to the aging priest Zacharias that Zacharias's wife, Elizabeth, would have a baby, Gabriel stood in the throne room of God receiving another commission to announce another miraculous conception. Sent to the tiny village of Nazareth, in the region of Galilee, Gabriel was to speak with a teenage girl, a virgin, whose name was Mary. She was betrothed to Joseph.

When Gabriel appeared to Mary, he extended God's grace to her, calling her "favored one" (Luke 1:28). Mary's response was bewilderment. Sensing her confusion and fear and perhaps knowing that the message he was about to deliver would complicate Mary's life forever, Gabriel repeated his greeting. Then he dropped the bombshell: the birth announcement of *the* King. "Mary, you have nothing to fear. God has a surprise for you: You will become pregnant and give birth to a son and call his name Jesus" (1:30–31 MSG).

Mary, though only a young girl, understood the basics of biology. Humanly speaking, the conception of a baby in a virgin's womb was impossible, but Gabriel assured Mary that nothing is impossible with God.

Mary couldn't understand why she had found such favor in God's eyes. She was a simple peasant girl in love with a simple carpenter. They would marry and children would come, but that was all in the future . . . or so she thought. And yet, there stood an angel of God bestowing *the* blessing, the wish every Jewish girl held in her heart—to be the mother of Messiah.

There, in the presence of God's messenger, she stood perplexed. All thoughts of sideways glances from neighbors, wagging tongues of village gossips, and questions from bewildered and doubtful family were someplace in a distant future. Those days and words would come and would wound her, but that day in humble submission she would trust God's word.

> Yes, I see it now:
> I'm the Lord's maid, ready to serve.
> Let it be with me
> just as you say. (1:38 MSG)

Mary saw herself as the humble servant of the Lord. She would—though it seemed so impossible—trust in the Word of God, spoken through the angel. And, regardless of the twists and turns ahead, she would submit her life to God's will. (DJ)

Oh, how tongues would wag when the marriage was moved up quickly. The older women would look with suspicion, since the wedding dress would have to be let out a little. Yet, Mary heard and Mary accepted because Gabriel reminded her, "Nothing is impossible with God."

—Chuck Swindoll

When Life Takes a RIGHT TURN

Some of the things God directs and permits in our lives feel like crushing blows. They fracture us and shatter our determination, persistence, and perseverance. But they are the tests that make us people of God.

Your seemingly impossible situation is unique to you. Other people's are unique to them. But *having* them is not unique. If you're not in an impossible situation now, you will be. At one time or another, we *all* will be. It's easy to lose heart in the midst of an impossibility. We're tempted to say, *I cannot handle this*. And the fact is, we can't.

But we know Someone who can.

The angel Gabriel, who said to Mary, "Nothing is impossible with God," was echoing the prophet Jeremiah when he said, "Ah Lord God! Behold, You have made the heavens and the earth by Your great power and by Your outstretched arm! Nothing is too difficult for You" (Jeremiah 32:17). God has never met His match; He never will. As Gabriel, who has stood in God's presence in worshipful praise since before human history began, said, "Nothing is impossible with God."

Nothing you could name is impossible for God. Nothing in your worry-filled world. Nothing that causes you restlessness through the night.

By the way, if you're in an impossible situation right now, consider *why* you are. You're not in this spot because you ran out of luck. There's no such thing as "luck"! You're not in a series of incredible circumstances that coincidentally fell together and caught God by surprise. He is never surprised! Let's be clear: you're here on purpose to be tested with the impossible.

What's more, God Himself knows what He intends to do. There's no knee-jerk afterthought with the Divine. He is worlds ahead of us. His perspective is beyond our lifetime. He has "the long view" of existence. We stand in this little pinpoint of time, but our God has His arms around it all. He knows exactly what He intends to do.

God wants to do His very best work when you are at the absolute end of your hope. We are all faced with a series of remarkable opportunities brilliantly disguised as impossible situations. Go forward in faith. As Mary did, say to God, "I am Yours. Do what you want."

—Charles R. Swindoll

A Surrendered HEART

As a young woman, missionary Betty Scott Stam wrote the following prayer of submission to God. Like Mary of Nazareth, Betty Stam was surrendering to God's plan regardless. In 1934, she and her husband John were martyred in China. Their deaths sparked a missionary movement all over the world which continues to impact Asia today.

Lord, I give up my own purposes and plans, all my own desires and hopes and ambitions . . . and accept Thy will for my life. I give myself, my life, my all utterly to Thee, to be Thine forever. I hand over to Thy keeping all of my friendships; all the people whom I love are to take second place in my heart. Fill me and seal me with Thy Holy Spirit. Work out Thy whole will in my life, at any cost. . . . To me to live is Christ. Amen![1]

In our endless search for strong, godly role models, we usually don't think to check out the local high school for prospective candidates. Yet the Bible often showcases exemplary young people whose hearts belonged to God and who gave up everything to follow Him. Despite crushing odds, biblical teenagers like Mary, Daniel, Joseph, and Josiah held their ground for God and stood firm, and often alone, in their faith.

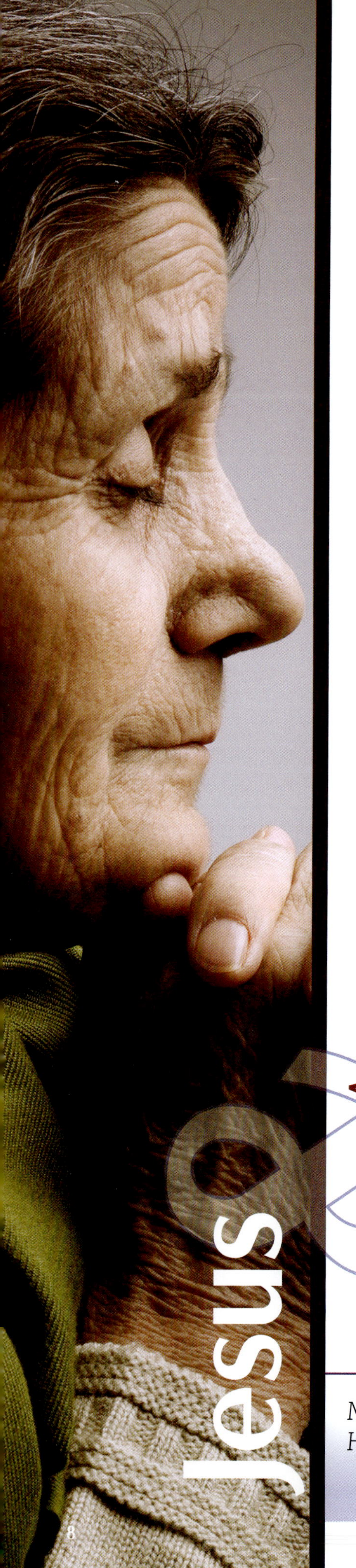

There was a prophetess, Anna the daughter of Phanuel, of the tribe of Asher. She was advanced in years and had lived with her husband seven years after her marriage, and then as a widow to the age of eighty-four. She never left the temple, serving night and day with fastings and prayers. At that very moment she came up and began giving thanks to God, and continued to speak of Him to all those who were looking for the redemption of Jerusalem.

—Luke 2:36–38

Grace

The Fullness of Joy

Her name means "gracious" and, as a pleasant coincidence, grace seems to have permeated her life. Anna, widowed as a young woman and with no children, faced a truly desperate future. But she refused to be defined by what she didn't have. What others saw as an empty life, Anna redefined as full.

During Anna's lifetime, Israel's political scene was in a terrible scramble. Early on, in 63 BC, Jerusalem had been taken over by the Romans. Perhaps this political crisis contributed to Anna's habit of fasting and praying in the temple. Either way, the habit was lifelong. And when Anna prayed, she lifted her hands to heaven, asking for the long-promised Messiah, who everyone envisioned would be Israel's political savior.

In her eighty-four years, Anna had seen Herod's extensive temple building project started and nearly completed. She had planted herself there at the temple, at the center of the busiest spot in the city, the very hub of Jewish life. She made it her home—choosing to be there worshiping rather than anywhere else brooding over how hard life was without a husband or children.

When her empty arms weren't lifted in prayer, they held other people's babies, played with other people's children, prayed for other people's families. As multiple generations turned, Anna was a fixture in this central place—fostering no bitterness for what she had not been given, only praising for how much she had and petitioning for what she hoped would come.

With one foot in the Old Testament and another in the New Testament, history unfolded right in front of Anna. It's almost too hard to imagine what that moment must have been like for Anna when she saw that young couple carrying their newborn boy across the temple portico. She knew right away who He was. She must have held out her empty arms to hold Jesus that day with her full heart bursting and her face tracked with joy.

What else could she offer to Mary and Joseph other than thanks to God? She had plenty to add later, though—telling every faithful one she met about the Baby in the temple and the hope He brought to the entire world. She *knew*. Her arms had held the Messiah. BP

No matter your age, no matter the odds — keep your sights on God and follow Him fully.

— Chuck Swindoll

What You Trade FOR YOUTH

ld and wise" is not necessarily a given. Old, you can't help. Wise is another matter. "Old and cranky" can just as easily be the alternative.

Old and wise women invest in, rather than just survive, the years. These strong, confident, deep women have seen their share of tragedy and lived to talk about it on the other side. And, in the end, they learned that God does all things well.

But that wisdom didn't just happen. It's no accident. The lines in their faces and the grey hair (under the color) are evidence of time invested in life. Angst or peace shows up between the laugh-lines.

Ask any woman who has walked with God more than thirty years, and she'll tell you godliness is a process, a series of choices. There's no such thing as instant insight. When you add hot water, you don't automatically get wisdom. Nothing takes the place of long conversations with God year after year. You learn that God has His own timetable, and He doesn't consult you on it. But He is trustworthy and good, and you can settle down in the faith of it. From the beginning of our walk with Christ right until the end, we never outgrow our need for His grace.

Martin Luther wisely said of aging:

> This life, therefore, is not righteousness but growth in righteousness; not health but healing; not being but becoming; not rest but exercise. We are not yet what we shall be, but we are growing toward it. The process is not yet finished, but it is going on. This is not the end but it is the road. All does not yet gleam in glory, but all is being purified.[2]

It makes you think: *would any of us trade the wisdom that we have now for the bodies we had way back when?*

Forget searching for the fountain of youth. Instead, take off your shoes and splash around in the fountain of joy. You're different from the young woman you once were—praise God for that. You've traded youth for wisdom, and you look marvelous! (BP)

WHAT EVERY GIRL NEEDS

At **15**, a girl needs good parents.
At **20**, a girl needs a good education.
At **25**, a girl needs a good opportunity.
At **30**, a girl needs good looks . . . or at least good bling.
At **40**, a girl needs good "support."
At **50**, a girl needs a good vacation.
At **60**, a girl needs good makeup.
At **70**, a girl needs a good sense of humor.
At **75**, a girl needs a good filter.
At **80**, a girl needs a good life story.

At every age, a girl needs good friends, hope, and a faith in God that grows deeper with age.

Think about it:
Knowing what you know now, what would you tell yourself at 25 years old about how to live wisely ?

Widows were a vulnerable group in biblical times. Their lives were defined by what they lacked. They had no inheritance rights and little opportunity to make a living. Their survival was at the mercy of their children, and if they had no children, the community. The law made some allowances to provide for widows, but it fell to God's people to ensure their care.

God's heart is tender toward women who are alone (Psalm 146:9). Exodus 22:22–24 warns anyone who would abuse them. In the book of Ruth, God pictured the desperate situation of three widows to illustrate His redeeming love for all people. The early church singled out widows as worthy of special attention and provision (1 Timothy 5:9–10; James 1:27).

Jesus was particularly mindful of the widow's plight. Counter to the culture, He *noticed* them and treated them as a gentleman should, with courtesy and respect. Even with His dying breath from the cross, He looked after the care of His own widowed mother (John 19:26–27).

Embracing Seasons

Donna Jones

As vice president of Living Bridge Media, Donna is the one to thank for coordinating what you hear on *Insight for Living* every day. She leads the creative team of broadcast and video editors and works with Chuck and Cynthia Swindoll on developing the programs and their on-the-air lineup. A veteran member of the Insight for Living team, Donna has served in leadership roles around the ministry for more than fifteen years. Donna enjoys life in Texas's hill country as a newlywed.

A Peek inside Insight for Living

"Ministry happens within our walls as well as throughout the world. I have grown spiritually so much through my time and experiences at Insight for Living. Chuck and Cynthia have always provided the environment for me to stretch and wrestle with the things that God wants to work on in me."

Is Christian Broadcasting Still Relevant?

"Absolutely. I came to Christ through *Insight for Living* and other broadcast ministries, and every day we hear that same testimony repeated from our listeners—who, by the way, cover the planet. Our best records indicate that *Insight for Living* is heard on every continent by a potential of millions a day. The intimacy of the relationship that radio and webcasting provides is all part of God's plan of getting His Word out . . . and changing lives (like mine)."

One Thing I've Learned

"Women go through many seasons through the years. Embrace each one for its unique gift—especially the season you're in today. Life goes so fast!"

What Does Hardship Teach You about God?

"God will reveal Himself through my circumstances when I wait on His timing. Whenever I move ahead of Him, it doesn't go well."

One of Donna's Favorite Verses

Therefore, having been justified by faith, we have peace with God through our Lord Jesus Christ, through whom also we have obtained our introduction by faith into this grace in which we stand; and we exult in hope of the glory of God. —Romans 5:1–2

Once you get a taste for cruising, you'll be spoiled for life.

All the amenities of a fine resort, more freedom, less hassle . . . no stress. A cruise is truly a dream vacation. And when you cruise with Insight for Living, you get even more. You get to be a part of a family.

We meet for fun and meaningful times together in God's Word with Chuck Swindoll. Special guest artists and top entertainers bless us with their talent. And of course, our days are capped off with more laughter and heart-warming connections than most experience in years.

There is also time that is all yours. Explore ports of call. Dig into new cultures and history. Dine like never before. Enjoy one great excursion after another. Or stay onboard! Lie back, be pampered, and let your cares float away.

A luxurious cruise with your hosts Chuck and Cynthia Swindoll is the perfect combination of a spiritual retreat and an expertly planned vacation. Take advantage of the worry-free service and quality—all with Insight for Living's stamp of approval. You and your family will make memories you'll talk about for years to come.

Discover the details for the next Insight for Living cruise at www.insight.org/events. CONFERENCES & TOURS

> *Then [Jesus] got up and left the synagogue, and entered Simon [Peter's] home. Now Simon's mother-in-law was suffering from a high fever, and they asked Him to help her. And standing over her, He rebuked the fever, and it left her; and she immediately got up and waited on them.*
>
> —Luke 4:38–39

Jesus & Peter's Mother-in-Law

Gratitude

Motivation for Service

What would you do if someone saved your life? No doubt you would be grateful. But would you devote your life to that person?

Peter's mother-in-law did.

The day may have started out as any other Sabbath. Peter, her son-in-law, was off work and over at the synagogue with his brother, Andrew; the brothers, James and John; and a young rabbi from Nazareth, Jesus. She was tending to her duties at home when suddenly everything changed. She felt feverish. Her skin burned as if it was on fire, but she shivered with chills. Could it be malaria? It wasn't unheard of. Maybe some other deadly disease? Whatever it was, Peter's mother-in-law retreated to her bed, too ill to move.

The men returned to Peter's house for lunch to discuss the ministry of Jesus. At the door, they were met not with the rich aroma of cooking fish and fresh bread but with the rancid stench of sickness. The entire household was in distress. Peter had already seen Jesus do some amazing things that day . . . could He help his mother-in-law?

Jesus stood over his friend's loved one, took her hand, and commanded the fever to leave her. Immediately—and amazingly—her forehead cooled, the sweating stopped, and she got up from her bed.

Returning to the kitchen, she finished the preparations for the meal and served Jesus with great delight.

Jesus comes to the soul-sick in quiet, slipping into the inner room where the soul burns under the fever of sin. He never bursts through doors demanding to heal anyone, but if invited, He is ever ready to take "our infirmities and carr[y] away our diseases" (Matthew 8:17). When Jesus enters our lives and heals us from the disease of sin, it is fitting that we thank and praise Him. But that is only the beginning. We should also emulate Peter's mother-in-law and *serve* Him. A heart overflowing with gratitude spills out through the fingers of service. DJ

We take the gift of eternal life with words of gratitude: "Thank You for forgiving me. Thank You for cleansing me. Thank You for the gift of eternal life." Then we have the joy of showing our gratitude by serving Him.

—Chuck Swindoll

CULTIVATING A GRATEFUL LIFE

"I have more blessings than problems."

The most enjoyable, approachable women you know are the ones who are grateful for the lives God has given them . . . and they don't mind telling you about it. They're not the ones who have the fewest problems or perfect pasts or all the expected reasons for being glad. They're simply the ones who choose to be grateful. And the Lord keeps them occupied with the "gladness" in their hearts (Ecclesiastes 5:20).

This mind-set is no small feat. Everything about life runs counter to living gratefully—especially as we get older and the temptation increases to be cynical, negative, brittle, bitter, isolated, self-focused, and whiny. Ingratitude is a battle raging in all of us, a struggle we rarely admit—a relentless war that's fought in silence and is shrouded in secrecy. A woman who cultivates gratitude attacks that enemy with aggressive intent.

A thankful woman counts her blessings. She "forget[s] none of [God's] benefits" (Psalm 103:2). She acknowledges that God surrounds her with His lovingkindness. He protects her. He heals her. He meets her needs morning, noon, and night. She is aware that God is on the throne. In quiet moments she realizes, *God is in me and moving me in His direction*. And the thought of this truth fills her with a quiet reverence for God and a joy in living.

How do you choose this kind of attitude? How can you combat a natural tendency toward ingratitude?

Exercise it. Put your attitude of gratitude to work every day. Try this: commit just a few minutes each day to record five things you're grateful to God for from *that day*. Make it a daily habit in the same time and place. Over time, you'll see gratitude becoming a more natural response in your life. Some days will be easier than others, but whenever your gratitude tank runs low, go back and read your daily lists of blessings. Page after page. Instance after instance. You'll find tangible reasons to be thankful as you look for God's good hand holding up your life. You are guaranteed to have more blessings than problems any day. BP

What Every Woman SHOULD HAVE

- Something perfect to wear if the interview or date of your dreams is an hour away
- A set of screwdrivers, a cordless drill, and the confidence to use them without help
- One friend who always makes you laugh, one who'll tell you the truth, and one who lets you cry
- An easy-to-read Bible and a notebook to write down what you're learning
- A good piece of furniture not previously owned by anyone else in your family
- A healthy sense of humor about life's imperfections (including your own)
- A recipe for a meal that will make your guests feel honored
- A movie or book that gives you a beautiful mental vacation
- A pair of stylish yet comfortable high heels and a bottle of your "signature" perfume
- A list of life goals and a step-by-step plan to reach them

Almost everyone in Capernaum worked in one of the town's two main industries: the military or fishing. Peter was a partner in a fishing business. More than likely, when Peter's mother-in-law prepared the meal for Peter and Jesus, she served them a signature fish lunch. Today, you can order "St. Peter's fish" (tilapia) at any local Galilee eatery.

The Samaritan woman said to Him, "How is it that You, being a Jew, ask me for a drink since I am a Samaritan woman?" (For Jews have no dealings with Samaritans.) Jesus answered and said to her, "If you knew the gift of God, and who it is who says to you, 'Give Me a drink,' you would have asked Him, and He would have given you living water."

—John 4:9–10

Jesus & The Samaritan Woman

Thirsty

A Conversation at a Well

To all women who are in a restless pursuit of love—who perhaps have compromised their values or settled for less: do you wonder if anyone could really love you?

Meet Jesus at the well.

It was high noon on a hot day. Jesus waited at Jacob's Well for the lone woman making her way up the deserted path. No one went to the well in the heat of the day. Jesus had sent His Twelve into town for food just so the conversation between Him and this woman could be private. She was a woman on the bad side of a moral decision, caught up in a sinful situation . . . and the whole town knew it. The dry Middle Eastern wind could have blown right through her broken spirit.

It shocked her that Jesus spoke to her—a righteous Jew addressing a woman! And a Samaritan at that! And He asked *her* for a drink when they both knew *she* was dying of spiritual thirst. She had drunk from all that the world had offered and ended up with a mouthful of sand.

With pitcher poised, she turned and dared to lift her eyes to meet His as He spoke, "Whoever drinks of the water that I will give him shall never thirst" (John 4:14). She gave Him water . . . He offered her eternal life.

Could He be the longed-for Messiah? She would need proof.

Then He told her everything she had done in her search for love. Painful, private things.

How did You know that?

But He said it all without shaming her—an acceptance she was unaccustomed to. She had never known this kind of transparency—love that saw her so truthfully and spoke so honestly and still offered mercy so freely.

When the disciples rejoined Jesus, they brought Him lunch. However, when the Samaritan woman told people about the love she had found at the well, she brought Him the whole town.

Ever wonder if you could be loved like that? You can. Do more than just meet Jesus—get to know Him. BP

As you slip out of bed each morning, thank God for His love and His calm, fresh reminders that this new day is under His control. Quietly state the encouraging truth: God loves me.

—Chuck Swindoll

Looking for LOVE

Everyone longs to be loved by somebody — to have a deep, devoted relationship with another person. God created us with that need for intimacy. But He never meant for any earthly relationship to be the center of our lives — that place is reserved for Him alone.

God created us in such a way that our souls feel complete only when we find our greatest satisfaction in Him. That's why early in His Word He tells us to "love the LORD . . . with all your heart and with all your soul and with all your might" (Deuteronomy 6:5). Not only does loving God first and best bring Him glory, it brings us the greatest joy.

God loves you.

Pause to consider all that means. He loves you like a groom loves a bride, like a father loves his child, like an artist loves his masterpiece. No one knows you better — all your secrets, all your faults, all the peculiarities that only a Lover can know.

His love doesn't depend on your loveliness but on His character. His love isn't at risk when you fail because it doesn't depend on you. He loves you because that's what He is: love. You are the beneficiary of this grace. All He asks is that you put Him first. That you please Him first. That you make your relationship with Him *the* priority of your life. And when you do, He promises that all your other relationships will be more satisfying.

Look for His love in the details of your life — you'll discover His love is the magnet, drawing you to Himself in all times and places. BP

From the Psalms

God's Love for You Is . . .

Protective (5:11)

Sweeter than honey (19:10)

Deeper than the ocean (86:13)

Unconditional (91:14)

Demonstrative (116:1)

Deeply personal (139:17)

Longer than a lifetime (145:20)

YOURS

Because women are made to be responders in romantic relationships, not initiators, to us belongs the waiting — which means placing our trust in Him who loves us, does all things well, and promises to crown us with everlasting joy. It means continued obedience in whatever God has given us to do today without allowing our longing for human love to shift our focus away from Him. Believe God is at work in your life, and be satisfied.

A woman's work is never done . . .

The writer of Proverbs wasn't kidding when he said that the virtuous woman "rises also while it is still night" and "does not eat the bread of idleness" (31:15, 27). A woman in Jesus's day worked hard from before dawn until after dark.

Women drew fresh water from the local well or spring twice a day, usually early in the morning and in the evening to avoid the heat. These were also social events. Together at the well, women would exchange news, gossip, and stories while they drew their families' water.

No wonder the Samaritan woman drew her water at noon. Perhaps she chose to endure the heat of the sun rather than the other women's blistering comments and glares.

Jesus said to her, "Woman, where are they? Did no one condemn you? . . . I do not condemn you, either. Go. From now on sin no more."

—John 8:10–11

Rescued

Caught . . . and Released

Early one morning, Jesus was teaching in the outer courts of the temple. A group of angry scribes and Pharisees interrupted the Lord's lesson, dragging a woman before Him and His listeners.

She had been caught in the very act of adultery, making her the perfect bait for their attempt to trap Jesus. Their trap came in the form of a loaded question:

"Now in the Law Moses commanded us to stone such women; what then do You say?" (John 8:5). Of course, they didn't really care about Jesus's opinion. As on other occasions, they merely hoped to find some means of trapping Jesus with His own words (Mark 12:13; Luke 20:20).

The Jewish leaders presented Jesus with a thorny question. The Law of Moses condemned adulterers to be stoned publicly (Deuteronomy 22:22–24). But Roman law prohibited the Jews from stoning anyone without permission. If He honored God's law, Jesus would incur the wrath of Rome. If He submitted to Roman law, Jesus would have to ignore the law of God. It seemed to them a perfect setup!

Refusing to take the bait, Jesus stooped over and began writing in the sand with His finger. Whatever He wrote had little effect on the frowning accusers. They kept pressuring Him for an answer. Eventually, Jesus stood to His feet and issued a challenge in one sentence: "He who is without sin among you, let him be the first to throw a stone at her" (John 8:7–8).

Jesus then resumed His writing in the dirt. You could have heard crickets chirping.

One by one—oldest first—the hypocritical judges dropped their rocks and slithered away. Only Jesus remained before the woman. The two-faced judges could not condemn, and the sovereign Judge refused to do so in light of His grace. He straightened up and spoke.

"'Woman, where are they? Did no one condemn you?' She said, 'No one, Lord.' And Jesus said, 'I do not condemn you, either. Go. From now on sin no more'" (8:10–11).

Jesus has that prerogative. He did not come to condemn the lost, but to save them by taking all condemnation for sin on Himself (3:16–17).

As with this woman, may His grace toward us become our motivation to live a life of obedience (Romans 12:1–2; Titus 2:11–14).[3]

—Charles R. Swindoll

Our shame screams loudly and our guilt is heavy. We convince ourselves we're not useful. We think we cannot measure up. We think, "I have to be somebody special to be useful or important to God." But the fact is, He does some of His best work with those who think they are finished.

—Chuck Swindoll

Am I FORGIVEN?

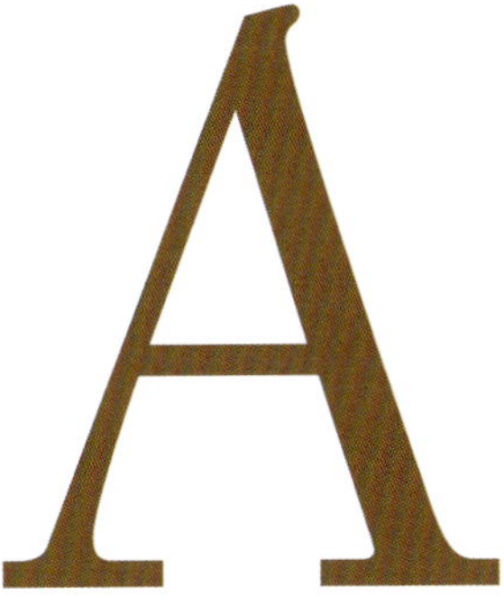

As a follower of Christ, you might experience a time in your life when you don't feel like your sin has been forgiven by God no matter what others tell you or what you know to be true about His forgiveness and grace. Perhaps you think your sin is too big. Or maybe you don't think you're worthy of the pardon. Perhaps you've sinned like this before and you think God may have drawn the line this time. You could read a long list of Bible verses and still not think they apply to you.

What you know to be true in your head hasn't made it yet to your heart. To make matters worse, you may feel the subject of your sin is far too sensitive to talk about with anyone who could perhaps help. So instead of feeling the freedom of forgiveness that Jesus paid the price to provide, you carry around the nagging burden of guilt. And when your church sings about the wonderful grace of God, you hold back and wonder if God could really reach you after all.

You just feel guilty. What should you do?

How we deal with our sin defines us.

When you see your sin, allow yourself to be heartbroken about it. Deal with it *God's way*. Agree with Him on the severity of your actions. Ask His forgiveness and then welcome His deepest work within you. Choose sincerity over ritual. Choose repentance over rationalization. Choose brokenness over boasting. Choose a right relationship with Him over your own pride. Choose His forgiveness over holding on to the burden of your sin.

God waits for that moment when He sees you turn around. He loves you, and when He sees your repentant heart, He runs to you. He lavishes you with His mercy and grace. He frees you to start again.

This could be your moment right now. 

What Did Jesus Write in the Sand (John 8:6)?

Nobody knows. Some suggest He scribbled the sins of the accusing Pharisees.

Scripture doesn't tell us what Jesus wrote, only what He said: "He who is without sin among you, let him be the first to throw a stone at her" (John 8:7).

Jesus uncovered the accusers' hearts and left them exposed. Any man who threw a stone would've implied that he was without sin. The only person qualified to throw a stone at the woman was the One who set her free.

Jesus flipped the mirror around and let the Pharisees get a good look at themselves . . . and what they saw wasn't pretty. One by one they dropped their stones and walked away.

In Bibles printed today, the account of the woman caught in adultery begins with John 7:53 and continues through 8:11. However, she does not appear at all in the earliest manuscripts, and later copies include the account in various places. Complicating matters even more, the vocabulary and style of this passage do not match the rest of John's gospel. Some suggest this incident may have occurred and been preserved in some form outside of Scripture, only to be included in the Bible much later. However, the likelihood of that possibility is questionable, considering the length of time between the first and sixth centuries, when it appeared in manuscripts with a special notation indicating the scribes' doubt. Many fine Christian scholars consider the story authentic because the consensus of church history has judged it worthy and because nothing in the story contradicts other teaching.[4]

Lifestyle Love

Maggie Gulliford

As a graphic artist at Insight for Living, Maggie adds life to the words on a page. She is so grateful for a job that gives her the flexibility to pursue the exciting opportunities God gives her. She has been living in the Dallas, Texas, refugee community for over a year, and loves it. In addition to doing a girls Bible study and helping run a Bible camp in the park, Maggie loves just spending time with her neighbors, eating meals, helping the kids with their homework, playing games, and baking *a lot* of cookies!

Whatever

"Getting to know God is worth wherever it leads you and whatever it costs."

On Being a Woman

"I like knowing that God made me who I am and how I am on purpose."

A Must

"Coke, not Pepsi."

God Uses Women Who Are . . .

" . . . breathing. Really—God can use anyone. I love what 1 Corinthians 1 says about the kinds of people God uses!"

One Word for Women

"Rest. Life is full of things that only God can do. Trying to do them yourself will only cause trouble. It's better to be still and wait."

One of Maggie's Favorite Verses

Wait for the Lord;
Be strong and let your heart take courage;
Yes, wait for the Lord. —Psalm 27:14

The Web is not about convenience anymore—it's about lifestyle. That's why Insight for Living has designed a new mobile Web site exclusively for use with a smart phone: **mobile.insight.org**. This site's clear, condensed format lets you navigate quickly to popular features such as Chuck Swindoll's daily devotionals, today's broadcast, free MP3s, and more. If you're one who takes the Internet with you in your pocket, bookmark this new, adapted version of our Web site!

mobile.insight.org

[Jesus] went to a city called Nain. . . . Now as He approached the gate of the city, a dead man was being carried out, the only son of his mother, and she was a widow; and a sizable crowd from the city was with her. When the Lord saw her, He felt compassion for her, and said to her, "Do not weep."

—Luke 7:11–13

Compassion

A Time to Live

She had a name, but it was erased by time. She had a husband, but his time had run its course. She had a son, but he had met an untimely end. She had a future, but the times were lonely, desperate, and bleak.

But *her* time hadn't run out.

What this widow didn't know was that on the day of her only son's funeral, a prophet even greater than Elijah, who had raised the dead son of the widow of Zarephath (1 Kings 17:8–24), was coming to her village.

Followed by His disciples and a large entourage, Jesus approached the village gate of Nain, just a few miles from His hometown of Nazareth, and witnessed the funeral procession. What caught Jesus's eye wasn't the body on the bier but the desperate moans of the widowed mother. Unannounced and unasked but prompted by compassion, Jesus approached the widow. "Do not weep" (Luke 7:13).

Jesus laid His hand on the plank bearing the body and the pallbearers suddenly stopped, halting the whole procession. Jesus then turned to the lifeless body and said, "Young man . . . Get up" (7:14 MSG). And like a spring wound tightly and suddenly released, the young man sprang up and began talking!

Wouldn't you like to know what the young man said? Better still, wouldn't you like to know what his mother thought when Jesus helped her son off of the stretcher and brought him to her? Imagine what must have passed through her mind!

We know what the people in the funeral procession thought: "A great prophet has arisen among us! . . . God has visited His people!" (7:16). The One who created time had stopped it before their very eyes.

The Lord of life and death had demonstrated His deep compassion for a desperate widow. She received back her son, and her future was secure. Her son would inherit her husband's estate and would care for her until it was her own time to be carried out of the village followed by a procession of mourners. (DJ)

Are you dealing with a situation as good as done, finding yourself in grief and without hope? When Jesus steps in, hope is always revived. A widow's only son died and was brought back to life. Where are you in that story?

—Chuck Swindoll

WHAT TO DO WHEN THE DOOR SLAMS SHUT

You've waited; you've sought godly counsel; you're continuing to pray. Your heart is willing, your spirit is ready, and your soul is longing. And about the time you get near the answer, *BANG!* . . . the door slams shut.

- You prayed for someone you love to be healed—and that person died this afternoon.
- You prayed for a job opportunity that embodied the hope of a new start—and you just heard that someone else got it.
- You prayed for the house to sell—and now it's in foreclosure.

Now what? What do you do with your faith now?

It is easy to be disillusioned and discouraged and to think you've missed God's instruction, when, in fact, you are in the very nucleus of His will. It is agonizing to have dreams dashed; to have hopes unfulfilled; to face a future that is unknown, unfamiliar, and sometimes, if the truth were known, unwanted. But God has a way of guiding us unerringly onto the path of righteousness for His name's sake.

Wherever today finds you—whatever wounds you may still be nursing and however deep the pit you're in—our Savior is deeper still. He's made no mistake. Your slammed door is what He planned and/or allowed—including the wrongs, the unfair treatment, and the losses. It's possible you may have been trusting God for an outcome instead of trusting God. Take heart; He is faithful.

Perhaps you've come to a closed door, and you've been pushing against it. It's hard for you to accept the fact that the door is truly shut tight. Stop the fight and let it be. Ask the Lord to meet with you as you consider the new possibilities of faith. You don't know what waits for you behind another door. Ask Him to give you peace in a whole new direction. And be open to it.[5]

—*Charles R. Swindoll*

Moving On, *One Step at a Time*

There's no formula for healing, but a few steps are common to all.

Keep living.
Eating, sleeping, breathing—they're taken for granted when things are good, forgotten when they're bad. Keep up healthy habits, and surround the littlest things with gratitude.

Open your eyes.
A door slammed, a person lost, a heart broken—they feel better if we don't look. Unfortunately, they don't *get* better on their own. Stop ignoring, minimizing, and denying the truth. Accept it.

Do the hard work.
Everybody gets hurt; not everybody gets over it. Do your part—grieve, get angry, say what's needed, feel at your depths. Ask others for help, and watch God work.

Look for the redemption.
God works for good; He *will* make all things new. Today is part of the process. Don't miss it.

Live fully.
Healed doesn't mean scar-free; it means wiser, purer, stronger. Leave old wounds behind—let go. Live today with all your refined heart.

In Jesus's time, on the same day that loved ones died, you buried them. You closed their eyes, washed their bodies, dressed them in their favorite clothes, and then wrapped them with linen bands, tucking spices in the folds of the linens to delay the smell of death. Then the bodies were laid on a bier and carried to the cemetery on the shoulders of pallbearers before being placed in a tomb.

This processional from home to the burial place was an immediate transition for the grieving, though mourning could last for a year. The family, along with professional mourners, alerted the town to their loved one's death with loud wailing and weeping as they followed the body to the tomb.

And there was a woman in the city who was a sinner; and when she learned that He was reclining at the table in the Pharisee's house, she brought an alabaster vial of perfume, and standing behind Him at His feet, weeping, she began to wet His feet with her tears, and kept wiping them with the hair of her head, and kissing His feet and anointing them with the perfume. Now when the Pharisee who had invited Him saw this, he said to himself, "If this man were a prophet He would know who and what sort of person this woman is who is touching Him, that she is a sinner."

—Luke 7:37–39

Forgiven

Lesson at a Dinner Party

"Party-crasher" was hardly the worst name she had ever been called. The others were far more biting: harlot, whore, prostitute. No one grows up aspiring to such a vocation. And no one outlives it.

It's better than starving, some would justify. She wasn't so sure. But when circumstances turned on her, selling what should have been treasured was the only way she knew to survive. Yes, she recognized who she had become. And she was haunted by what it had cost.

She also knew something that the men in that room seemed to have forgotten. The label "sinner" has no gradient scale. No best-to-worst or forgivable-to-unforgivable. There is just one measure: forgiven or not. On some, most likely recent, day she had found forgiveness in the eyes of the Messiah, her Savior, Jesus.

So never mind the rude chatter that swept the room; Jesus heard her heart. *Thank You, Jesus. Thank You for rescuing me. Thank You for bending down to hear my cry when no one else dared or cared. Thank You for taking my beaten up, broken life and not patching it up—but making it new.*

Forgiveness: received. The beauty of it made her weep.

And He didn't stop her. Jesus knew everything about her. He knew exactly what "kind of woman she was," and it moved Him even more. "Her sins, which are many, have been forgiven" (Luke 7:47). And then in response, her love for Him overflowed . . . in tears, in gratitude, in sacrifice, in worship. She used to be bought cheap; now she understood, at least in small part, that she had been bought back, redeemed by forgiveness. And the only appropriate place to be at that moment was at His feet. Broken, new, worshiping, adoring. A living, breathing, weeping picture of grace. BP

Think back over this past week, then this past month. Think of what life would have been like if the Lord had not forgiven you. Think back from the day you accepted the Lord Jesus until this moment. Never forget what it was like under the guilt of sin. And never forget that as you have brought your sin to Him each day, He has continued to cleanse you with the eternal detergent. It washes away sin at the mere mention of the word.

—Chuck Swindoll

HOW CAN I CLEAN UP THIS MESS?

No matter how you look at it, sin is dirty—filthy dirty. Something inside each of us wants to deny it, *Oh, it's just a little dust*, and sweep it under the rug. But God says there's no way to deal with sin other than washing it clean. The problem is that we don't have a detergent strong enough to clean up our own mess.

There was once a filthy, helpless man lying in the streets of a city that Jesus was visiting. The man knew his own desperate condition. He also knew Jesus could help. So when Jesus was within earshot, the man yelled out, "'Lord, if You are willing, You can make me clean.' And [Jesus] stretched out His hand and touched him, saying, 'I am willing; be cleansed'" (Luke 5:12–13).

Jesus's hands touched dirty and desperate people that day. And soon after, those same hands were pinned to a cross—His own blood pouring from the wounds. Medical professionals tell us that blood is the finest of all detergents. More than any other ingredient, blood does the greatest work of cleansing our bodies from the inside out, keeping us alive and free from contamination. How appropriate that God says Jesus's blood *cleanses* the willing heart from all sin (1 John 1:7).

Jesus's blood scrubs our willing hearts clean—from the inside out. When we admit our desperately dirty condition and cry out to God, Jesus stretches out His nail-scarred hand and touches us. He is forever willing to take a filthy heart and bathe it in His blood—making it cleaner than it's ever been.

No matter how dirty you are—God's forgiveness can wash your soul spotless. BP

GRADING SIN ON A CURVE

Too often we grade sin on a curve. Do any of these statements come out of your mouth or into your mind?

- *Sure, I sin, but at least I don't ________.*
- *Well, it needed to be said . . .*
- *No, it wasn't the best thing to do, but given the circumstances . . .*
- *I chose the better of two evils.*
- *But I was angry . . .*

When we say these things, we minimize our sin. Let the Spirit hold up a mirror to you and show you where you miss the mark. First John 1:8–9 says, "If we say that we have no sin, we are deceiving ourselves and the truth is not in us. If we confess our sins, He is faithful and righteous to forgive us our sins and to cleanse us from all unrighteousness."

What can wash away my sin?
Nothing but the blood of Jesus;
What can make me whole again?
Nothing but the blood of Jesus.

Oh! precious is the flow
That makes me white as snow;
No other fount I know,
Nothing but the blood of Jesus.[6]

Washing someone's feet was a customary honor shown to guests in Jesus's day. The roads were made of dirt, and walking was the primary means of transportation. No doubt cool water not only provided cleanliness but also soothed and comforted guests' tired feet. This menial duty was performed by the servant in the house or the person of the humblest status.

The woman in Luke 7 took this foot-washing service a step further. Everything about her act was humble, respectful, and adoring . . . and Jesus appreciated the significance of every nuance.

Her act of love shows up in deep contrast with the pride of the host who didn't miss the nerve of this "sinner woman" and judged Jesus's supposed cluelessness . . . yet strangely missed the depravity of his own heart.

> *Now after He had risen early on the first day of the week, He first appeared to Mary Magdalene, from whom He had cast out seven demons.*
>
> *—Mark 16:9*

Delivered

A Life Transformed

Her name is as well-known as any apostle's.

Yet the truth about her life often lies shrouded behind myths, fiction, and flat-out conjecture. Modern art and bestselling novels paint her as everything from the infamous woman caught in adultery to the wife of Jesus. But Scripture portrays a different person altogether.

She was called Magdalene, likely to distinguish her from the other Marys mentioned in the Gospels (Luke 8:2). Her name reveals that she hailed from Magdala, a town along the western shore of the Sea of Galilee.

How seven demons came to enter Mary Magdalene is unknown . . . but how they left her, the Gospels make clear—Jesus drove them out (Mark 16:9).

Mary's deliverance from demonic possession no doubt ignited her devotion to the ministry of Jesus. Along with other women Jesus healed, Mary followed the Lord and supported His ministry from her personal financial means (Luke 8:2–3).

As one of Christ's followers, Mary heard what the disciples heard. She saw the miracles. She ate the bread He multiplied. She accompanied Him to the feasts in Jerusalem—including the final Passover when the Jewish leaders arrested Jesus and condemned Him to death.

During the Lord's agonizing hours on the cross, Mary Magdalene stood nearby with a few others (John 19:25). She watched as Joseph of Arimathea took Jesus's body down from the cross, wrapped His corpse in linen, and laid it in Joseph's own tomb (Matthew 27:55–61).

Yet with all of Mary's devotion to the Lord, even she didn't expect what happened next.

Early Sunday morning, Mary accompanied some other women to Jesus's tomb in order to anoint His body. But the tomb was empty! Mary ran to Peter and told him that Christ's body had been taken away. Peter and John sprinted to the tomb, found it empty . . . and left amazed. Mary stood there alone, weeping . . . then she heard a voice.

"Woman, why are you weeping?"

Mary answered the man, "Sir, if you have carried Him away, tell me where you have laid Him, and I will take Him away" (John 20:15).

Jesus revealed His identity with one word: "Mary!" (20:16).

She knew His voice by heart. Amazingly, she had been given the honor of being the first person to witness Him after the resurrection . . . and to witness about Him to others.

Like Mary, we have the privilege to tell all who will listen that Christ is risen! Like Mary, Jesus has delivered our lives from the power of Satan so we may live in the power of His resurrection . . . anticipating, one day, our own (Acts 26:18; Philippians 3:10). WS

VOWS FOR THE **SINGLE WOMAN**

***F**or better or for worse,* *for richer, for poorer, in sickness and in health, for as long as we both shall live.*

The promises are as familiar as the white gown, fresh flowers, and the gooey-eyed couple who speak those vows in good faith and with conviction. That's good—because we all know there's ample reason why that *for better or for worse* part makes it into the script. It takes commitment to build a successful married life.

It also takes commitment to build a successful single life. Take the following commitments to heart as you pursue the unique calling God has given you.

For Better or for Worse

Commitment 1: I promise to see myself as a whole person and then act that way. Single does not mean "half," as in "half of a whole." A successful single woman approaches life from a "whole" mind-set. She takes to heart that she is "complete in Christ" (Colossians 1:28).

For Richer, for Poorer

Commitment 2: I promise to give of myself, my time, my finances, and my talents to invest in God's kingdom. Fear sometimes threatens a single woman's security and tempts her to hoard her resources. *Who will help me if I don't have enough*? A successful single woman knows God will provide for her in outrageous, only-God-could-do-that sort of ways (Philippians 4:19).

In Sickness and in Health

Commitment 3: I promise to treat self-pity like cancer. Detect it early, take its threat seriously, and get self-pity out of your life before it's allowed to grow. A successful single woman recognizes the temptation that singles naturally face: to think too often of themselves. She doesn't let her focus turn inward but sees her independence as making her available to serve others' needs (Romans 12:10–13).

For as Long as I Live

Commitment 4: I commit to living fully in "today" for the rest of my life. Forget the "When . . . then" syndrome. Don't let yourself say, "When I get married, then I'll entertain more." Or, "When I'm 'a couple,' then I'll take exciting vacations." Or, "When someone shares this home, then I'll do more with the décor." A successful single woman sees each stage and status of her life not as a liability but as a gift with unique freedoms and opportunities (1 Corinthians 7:7–8).

It is God's delight to present to the world a woman who finds her joy in being a precious and loved member of the bride of Christ. BP

How Are You Giving Your Life **AWAY**?

Think of specific ways you can share Christ with your world today.

Here are a few to get you started:

Practice random acts of love.

Notice and meet someone's need in your church or community.

Use your words for good.

Invest your time and/or money in a ministry that tugs at your heart.

Live as a person of grace and forgiveness.

The people of first-century Israel spent a large part of each day much as we do: working to earn their daily bread. Everyone worked. In fact, working quietly for one's living was, by Jewish tradition, a duty and a sign of greatness. A woman, whether married or single, would often choose to be, among other vocations, a domestic servant, a midwife, a shepherdess, a potter, a professional mourner, a scamstress, or a weaver.

What will you be like as a Christian ten years from now? Will you be walking with Christ, excited about His plan, serving Him in various capacities around the world? Or will you have taken your cue from the world's agenda and grabbed everything you can for yourself? You've followed too closely to believe that lie! Don't be afraid to trust the Lord with your future. He won't take advantage of your faith. In fact, He'll honor it!

—Chuck Swindoll

Grace for the Moment

Mary Graham

Insight for Living board of directors member Mary has visited every continent, most while serving on the staff of Campus Crusade for Christ International. Indeed, she has had a first-row seat to God at work in the lives of people all over the world. Mary now leads Live Events for Thomas Nelson Publishing Company, including *Women of Faith*, which hosts America's largest women's conference, and *The Revolve Tour* for teenage girls.

What Do Women of Faith Need?

"To understand God's grace! We try so hard to get everything right on our own and easily forget that God's grace is enough."

Purse Etiquette

"Everything in my purse is in a case. *Everything*. And most of the cases are black."

A Tip for Every Day

"Life is manageable in the moment. Don't worry about what was or what will be. God gives you grace for the moment."

I Have a Dream . . .

" . . . that the adventure I've enjoyed in my relationship with God since I was a college student will get me all the way home."

One of Mary's favorite Verses

"I am the vine, you are the branches; he who abides in Me and I in him, he bears much fruit, for apart from Me you can do nothing." —John 15:5

Uniquely Insight for Living—An Online Store of Trusted Resources

You heard a message today on *Insight for Living* that was exactly what you needed. You've got to have it. You've got to listen again. Where can you get it *today*? Go to **www.insight.org/store**.

Anything you hear on the radio or read about in a newsletter, you can get online at **www.insight.org/store**. In fact, almost *everything* you hear about from Insight for Living you can get in our online store. And with "What does Chuck teach about . . ." topic searches and convenient categories, finding what you need is easy.

Get your favorite resources and discover new ones from more than thirty years of ministry . . . all from the comfort and convenience of your own home!

insight.org / store

> *A woman who had a hemorrhage for twelve years, and could not be healed by anyone, came up behind Him and touched the fringe of His cloak, and immediately her hemorrhage stopped. And Jesus said, "Who is the one who touched Me?"*
>
> —*Luke 8:43–45*

Jesus & The Sick Woman

Healed

Faith on the Fringes

When you've been sick for a long time, you'll do almost anything to feel better. Even break the rules. For one woman perched on the edge of the crowd, any risk was worth the hope of healing.

She had already endured a dozen years of disappointment, suffering with an illness peculiar to women. What should have lasted five days each month had flowed for more than 4,380 days straight. One doctor after the next—not one of them could help her. A few, in fact, had hurt her. All of them drained her money. Now she was broke and getting worse.

What pained her more was the loss of human contact and the ugly label that defined her: "unclean." She was forbidden to join in the annual worship celebrations, to walk into the temple court, to light the Sabbath evening candles, to eat the Passover meal, forbidden even the touch of her husband. She lingered unwelcomed on the fringes of her former life. Exhausted, humiliated, and desperately alone.

No doubt news of a healer spread quickly in the hopeless community of the unclean.

What she had heard of this Jesus and His life-saving message had stirred faith in her—surprising, since everything good in her life had long ago drained out of her. She thought it would be enough if she could just touch Him . . .

So with the courage of the desperate, she pressed through the crowd, and in a way no one would notice, she simply touched the back of His shawl after He passed by . . . just the fringes.

Immediately she felt life flood her body. Warm, colorful, electric life. And the Healer whirled around, "Who touched Me?"

His tone was not accusatory—more like surprise. His power had responded to her faith, and He had felt it. Disregarding His impatient disciple, Jesus stopped and searched the crowd for the face of faith. And when their eyes met, He welcomed the audacity of her trusting reach. For it was this confidence, not superstition, that cured her—flooding her with a more generous and thorough healing than she had dared hope.

Best of all, He called her *daughter*. It had been a lifetime since anyone spoke to her with such tenderness. And He wished her *shalom*. Peace—that *wholeness* of life that comes from being brought into a right relationship with God. For the first time in twelve years—no, in her whole life—she was whole . . . and clean. BP

Circumstances that turn against us force dependence on God.
Circumstances that force dependence on God teach us patience.
Circumstances that teach us patience make us wise.

—Chuck Swindoll

JUST BREATHE

Sometimes, the new kind of normal is really just a search for the old kind of life. When you've been sick for a long time, you just want to feel better.

If only your health could improve, you'd bargain anything. If a trial or procedure promised relief, you'd risk it. If life could just return to normal . . .

No matter how big that "if" gets, you keep the hope of healing alive. Breathing, in and out. In and out. Because without hope, you'll stop being alive; then eventually you'll stop breathing.

But where does that hope come from? When tests and treatments have done their best, who restores your soul and helps you get up every morning in spite of the pain? That healing comes from an unexpected source.

Somewhere in the perseverance, there's a turning—when real life is no longer found in the sought-after relief but in a change of perspective. Most of the time, that kind of healing happens gradually. Sometimes it's not until years later that you realize you've healed in different parts of you. Other times, God knows your time is short; you need to understand right then. Either way, you get your life back.

Maybe not the pain-free, long life you dreamed about. But a deeper kind of life—a life accentuated by gratitude in spite of struggle, increased faith in God's working a bigger plan, and a stronger character soldered together with hard-won humility. And you realize you *are* better than you were before. Better because You know Christ better. Better because you understand the fellowship of His suffering better. Better because you've tasted just a bit of the power that raised Jesus from the dead.

And so, every morning and every evening and all the moments in between, you breathe in His life. Breathe in His hope. Breathe in His help. And in the very act of inhaling and exhaling, you discover His grace has become your life and breath. (BP)

Truth That Brings HEALING

We also rejoice in our sufferings, because we know that **suffering produces perseverance; perseverance, character; and character, hope**. And hope does not disappoint us.
—Romans 5:3–5 (NIV)

Therefore we **do not lose heart**. Though outwardly we are wasting away, yet inwardly we are being renewed day by day. For our light and momentary troubles are achieving for us an eternal glory that **far outweighs them all**.
—2 Corinthians 4:16–17 (NIV)

That I may know Him and the power of His resurrection and the fellowship of His sufferings, being conformed to His death.
—Philippians 3:10

In Jesus's day, Jewish men wore prayer shawls called *tallits*. (In fact, they still do!) The most important parts of the shawl are the long tassels on each corner, the *tzitzit*, knotted five times symbolizing the five books of Moses. The four spaces between these knots represent the letters of God's name, YHWH. The knots along the prayer shawls' edges use exactly 613 knotted strings, representing the 613 laws of the Torah.

Malachi prophesied that the Messiah would come with "healing in its wings" (4:2). The Hebrew word for "wings," *kanaph*, is also the word for "corners" or "borders" describing these long tassels. Based on this passage, the Jews expected the Messiah to have healing in His tassels.

The sick woman probably did not know this. Risking the consequences of the law that labeled her unclean and commanded that she shouldn't touch or be touched, she simply grasped at the last threads of Jesus's shawl as He walked by. (See Numbers 15:37–41; Malachi 4:2.)

One of the synagogue officials named Jairus came up, and on seeing Him, fell at His feet and implored Him earnestly, saying, "My little daughter is at the point of death; please come and lay Your hands on her, so that she will get well and live." And He went off with him. . . .While [Jesus] was still speaking, they came from the house of the synagogue official, saying, "Your daughter has died; why trouble the Teacher anymore?" But Jesus, overhearing what was being spoken, said to the synagogue official, "Do not be afraid any longer, only believe.". . . [Jesus] entered the room where the child was. Taking the child by the hand, He said to her, "Talitha kum!" (which translated means, "Little girl, I say to you, get up!"). Immediately the girl got up and began to walk, for she was twelve years old. And immediately they were completely astounded.

—*Mark 5:22–24, 35–36, 40–42*

Jesus & Jairus's Daughter

Prayer

Empty Hands Lifted Up

Desperation is often the first step toward grace.

So desperate was Jairus that he fell on his face in the sand, pleading for the life of his girl—his one and only daughter. Who doesn't know what a daughter can do to a daddy? He was no longer a proud official, looking proper and respectable. Jarius had become a humbled, broken man whose daughter was dying.

Time is of the essence when emergencies strike. And Jesus understood this man's pain. Without a word, He followed Jairus, and hope fired up again in Jairus's soul. He had seen what Jesus had done with blind men and the lame. He had heard of what had happened in Decapolis when that demoniac was delivered of demons. *Jesus can help. Surely He can do something for my little girl. I must get Jesus to her. And fast!*

But Jesus didn't seem to sense the urgency. He paused in the crushing, crowded street, turned, and asked the ridiculous, "Who touched me?" It was all Jairus could do to not pick Jesus up and carry Him home. *Let's go, Jesus! Don't you understand my daughter is dying?*

Blame it on the delay or the treacherous illness that stole his precious girl, but the sight of his servant in the crowd hijacked all Jairus's hope. The news was the worst a parent could hear: *trouble the Healer no longer; your daughter is dead.*

Urgency: over.

Who knows what Jairus thought when Jesus said, in effect, "Have no fear, Jairus, only believe" (Mark 5:36). Hope? Faith? Disbelief? Or perhaps nothing. Perhaps he was still numb from the devastating news: ". . . your daughter is dead." Nevertheless, Jesus cut through the crowd and the wail of the mourners at Jairus's house and went into the room that served as the crypt where the lifeless daughter lay.

She would have already turned cold. Her spirit had long-since departed. Her charm was gone. The 12-year-old girl no longer danced or played, laughed or sang. She was *gone* . . . until Jesus reached out and took her ashen, limp hand and spoke to her in her native Aramaic,"Talitha kum!" *Little girl, stand up!* Some suggest that the word *girl* could be rendered, "little lamb."

Her spirit returned to her. Her eyes opened and flashed with life. Her skin warmed. Without saying a word, she stood up.

Can you imagine the mother and daddy at that moment?

—*Charles R. Swindoll*

WHILE YOU W·A·I·T

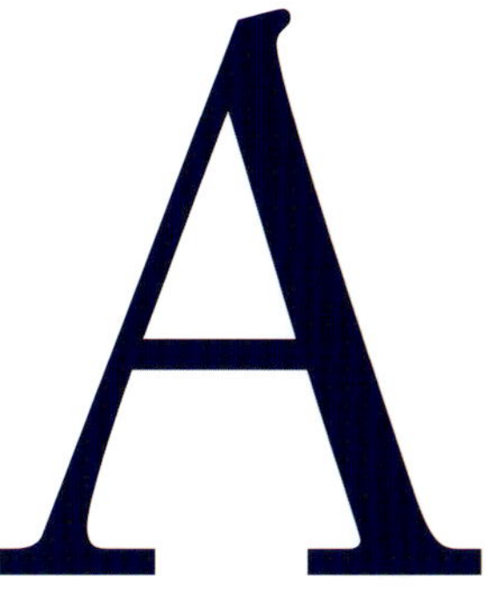

t times, waiting for an answer from God feels like driving an ambulance in a traffic jam. Turn the siren louder if you like, but the cars aren't moving. You can't get through.

Our lives are often marked by similar delays. We're in a hurry, but God is not. We pound heaven's door pleading for a response, and all we get is . . . silence.

What is God doing? The delay is a mystery to us.

The one who follows God by faith is always asked to wait. From the perspective of a lifetime, we can see that at least as important as what we wait for is the work God wants to do in us while we wait.

If we trust Him while we wait, God builds our confidence in His character. Learning to trust Him in the space between the need and the answer solidifies what we believe about Him. Over time, we become certain of His love—*He wants only what is best for us.* We stand by His wisdom—*He knows what is best for us.* We grow convinced of His power—*He is able to do what is best for us.*

God knows that it's hard for us to walk by faith, so He made some promises to assure us while we wait:

He's not going to leave us (Hebrews 13:5).

He'll redeem this situation for good (Romans 8:28).

He is working a bigger plan (1 Corinthians 2:9).

We may never know this side of heaven what God was up to while we waited. But no doubt, God will have been at work, fashioning a plan of such beauty and symmetry that our minds could not have received it.

We don't have to take our view of life only from what we can see or from what's happening right in front of us. We don't have to be imprisoned by the crazy doubts in our heads that we know aren't true. *Hang on to the things I've told you*, God has said (Psalm 103:1–22).

Continue to pray. Continue to wait. And in the meantime, believe that God is not only better than our fears, He's also better than our hopes. BP

WHAT KIND OF WAITER ARE YOU?

Give yourself points according to the following scale, then tally them to learn your waiting style.

1 = never | **3** = sometimes | **5** = nonstop

While waiting, how often do you:

___ Under- or overeat, overspend, over-talk

___ Become Ms. Fix-It

___ Worry and doubt

___ Whine or pitch a fit

___ Bark (or bite!)

___ Have a meltdown

Total: _______

1–10 You're an Elizabeth. In waiting, your faith grows. When it's over, you rejoice.
Her story: Luke 1
Encouragement for you: 1 Corinthians 15:58

11–20 You're a Mary or Martha. You don't doubt; you're just confused when God says, "Wait." You have big-picture trouble.
Their story: John 11:1–43
Encouragement for you: Romans 8:24–26

21–30 You're a Sarah. You know God's plans are good . . . but He takes too long! You take matters into your own hands.
Her story: Genesis 15–16; 18:1–15; 21:1–20
Encouragement for you: Psalm 25:3–5

In Jesus's day, when someone died, a loud and sorrowful wail announced it to the community. Because burial usually happened within the day, one of the only funeral preparations was to hire professional wailers who had mastered the art of mourning, which included playing flutes, beating their breasts, and grieving the dead with a wavering, shrill cry. Even the poorest family was expected to have at least one wailing woman and a flute.

A Canaanite woman from that region came out and began to cry out, saying, "Have mercy on me, Lord, Son of David; my daughter is cruelly demon-possessed." But He did not answer her a word. And His disciples came and implored Him, saying, "Send her away, because she keeps shouting at us."

But He answered and said, "I was sent only to the lost sheep of the house of Israel." But she came and began to bow down before Him, saying, "Lord, help me!" And He answered and said, "It is not good to take the children's bread and throw it to the dogs." But she said, "Yes, Lord; but even the dogs feed on the crumbs which fall from their masters' table." Then Jesus said to her, "O woman, your faith is great; it shall be done for you as you wish." And her daughter was healed at once.

—Matthew 15:22–28

Jesus & The Canaanite Woman

Satisfied

Crumbs from the Table

Nothing takes us to our knees faster than a sick child. Truth be told, we'll forget our own dignity as we attempt to find solace for our little one. We'll talk to complete strangers. We'll even beg. Anything.

It happened on a day when Jesus was trying to get away from the pressing needs of ministry. He took His disciples forty miles northwest into Gentile country. Surely, no one would know them there. But sure as shootin', there was a woman—just one—who recognized Him and whose persistent begging for help just about drove the disciples nuts. "Send her away, Lord. She's driving us crazy!" But the Lord didn't say a word.

Nothing made this Canaanite mother back off. She refused to shut up. She definitely wouldn't walk away. "Please, sir, please help me. My daughter is cruelly terrorized by a demon." This woman wasn't going home to her scared, horrified daughter without an answer.

Home: just imagine what a wreck it was. The family hadn't known a happy day since that demon had arrived. So this gutsy, risk-taker paid no attention to the long list of reasons that would have normally kept her away from the Lord. Instead, she kept pleading for help.

Then He finally answered her . . . but it wasn't what anyone expected: "It is not right to take the children's bread and toss it to the dogs" (Matthew 15:26 NIV).

What did Jesus say?

The response was so unlike Him. But the Lord had a motive: He was fishing for faith.

The mother was quick with a comeback and not at all offended. Humbly, and perhaps with raised eyebrows, she creatively used Jesus's own words to turn His attention to her desperation "You're right, Master, but even the puppies feed on the crumbs that fall from the table." What insight! What determination! What faith!

Jesus smiled. "Woman, your faith is great; it shall be done for you as you wish" (15:28). And then, after however long that demon had had control of her daughter, it was finally gone.

That day the Lord had two gifts in mind . . . one for that faith-filled Gentile family and another for His disciples: a lesson on great faith—taught in a land despised by the Jews through a Canaanite woman who cried out to God for the life of her child.

—Charles R. Swindoll

MEASUREMENTS AND CURVES

A **woman is often judged** by the things she can't control. She is measured by the way her body curves or doesn't curve—by inches and comparisons. She is measured by numbers—by age, zip code, tax bracket, and IQ. By letters—DWF, Mrs., Dr., CEO. She is measured by the outside things that don't add up to who she is on the inside.

Perhaps in our attempt to see where *we* stand, we put other people into categories. Someone always comes out a VIP, while others are pushed to the margins and ignored. And we end up somewhere near the top or at the very bottom.

But God doesn't grade on the curve; His grid is grace. He loves the world. Red and yellow, black and white—all are precious in His sight. From the one whose capacities are simple and scarred to the beauty and the scholar—we are created in His image, and we bear His fingerprints.

So rather than draw lines that divide people, God draws a circle to include every child, woman, and man that He created and says, "I love you." He sees that we all need saving. Across the circle, He draws the cross of Christ. And across the debt of our own making, God writes, in effect, "Paid in full" (Colossians 2:14).

Yet in love, God requires that we choose this gift. *Will I believe I am desperate without Christ and take His offer of salvation? Or will I leave the coupon on the floor and walk away? Will I choose to deceive myself into believing I can survive on my own?*

We choose life—fulfilled, beautiful life—not by comparing ourselves to others but by standing next to Christ. Once we admit our debt of sin that we can't do anything about and then turn to see Christ in all His reality, we have no problem seeing ourselves in the proper place—dearly loved but perhaps lower and smaller and quieter than we thought . . . and in desperate need of saving.

So if we are to be measured at all, let us be measured by what we can choose. We can choose to believe. We can choose to humble ourselves under God's hand and be saved and safe and fulfilled. BP

WHAT EVERY WOMAN SHOULD REMEMBER

Where you hid your mad money, the Snickers bar, and the spare keys to your house and car

Never post a photo on Facebook of you and your friend in swimsuits—even if you look fabulous

Be kind . . . everyone you meet is struggling with something

The name of your best lipstick, hair dye color, and the phone number of your family's favorite take-out

Something better is coming after this life

Your mother-in-law's birthday and your children's birth stories

Practice good posture and have a confident handshake and a winning smile

Keep a gratitude journal . . . because it's too easy to forget life's blessings

A tidy house and the number on the scale are not measures of your worth

God promises that He is always with you and will always love you

Q: *Why was there animosity between Israelites and Canaanites?*

A: This conflict was a long hatred. When the children of Israel came back from captivity in Egypt, the land was occupied by the Canaanites, a wicked people who worshiped a variety of heinous false gods and enticed Israel to join them. In the name of their gods, Baal and Molech, they did detestable things—like religious prostitution and child sacrifice as offerings to their idols. God hates any kind of idol worship and didn't want Israel distracted or deceived by this evil. His command to drive the Canaanites from the land was His judgment on their completely evil ways. A thousand years later in Jesus's time, this animosity still colored their relationships. Even then, Canaanites still lived in the land but only on the fringes.

A Balancing Act

Carmen Zavala Montgomery

Director of Insight for Living's Spanish-language ministry, *Visión Para Vivir*, Carmen loves how she's able to use her second language to communicate God's Word. Born and raised in Miami after her family emigrated from Honduras, Carmen now balances the rewarding challenges of a growing ministry with her busy (never boring!) life at home with her husband, Chad, and their active, enthusiastic boys, Coleman and Caleb.

What Do You Wish Women Knew?

"We each have a gift that God has given us. Do all you can to find out what it is and then put it to use. Be faithful!"

Your Best Accessory

"Red lipstick! I like the way it makes me feel."

What's in Your Purse?

"A case for my son's retainer. What can I say? A mom has to do what she can to enhance her boy's smile."

What Is a Passion God Has Given You for *Visión Para Vivir*?

"Enseñar la Palabra de Dios en una manera clara en el idioma de nuestro corazón."
(Teach God's Word in a clear way in the language of our heart.)

Don't Forget!

"God has a plan for me, and I have to follow Him every step of the way. God uses women who allow Him to lead. He will never disappoint."

One of Carmen's Favorite Verses

"For I know the plans that I have for you," declares the Lord, "plans for welfare and not for calamity to give you a future and a hope. Then you will call upon Me and come and pray to Me, and I will listen to you. You will seek Me and find Me when you search for Me with all your heart."
—Jeremiah 29:11–13

This is where history began. And where it will end . . . and begin again.

When you stand on the ground where the Bible's events took place, you're not just a tourist on an interesting vacation, you're a pilgrim on a journey of faith. From that day forward, every time you open your Bible, its pages will burst into full color. And when you experience Israel with Insight for Living, time and again you'll find yourself saying, *Oh! Now I understand!*

In the care of experienced, seasoned professionals, you'll travel the land with people you'll soon call friends. We'll stop at significant places along the way to get perspective from Scripture and learn important lessons from history. We'll walk and pray and sing together, inspired by magnificent surroundings. We'll experience moments—some planned, some impromptu—that will stay with us the rest of our lives.

Like the pilgrims of old, perhaps this is your time to say, "Next year in Jerusalem . . ."

Discover the details for the next Insight for Living Holy Land tour at www.insight.org/events. **CONFERENCES & TOURS**

Jesus & Mary of Bethany

> *Now when Jesus was in Bethany, at the home of Simon the leper, a woman came to Him with an alabaster vial of very costly perfume, and she poured it on His head as He reclined at the table. But the disciples were indignant when they saw this, and said, "Why this waste? For this perfume might have been sold for a high price and the money given to the poor." But Jesus, aware of this, said to them, "Why do you bother the woman? For she has done a good deed to Me. For you always have the poor with you; but you do not always have Me. For when she poured this perfume on My body, she did it to prepare Me for burial. Truly I say to you, wherever this gospel is preached in the whole world, what this woman has done will also be spoken of in memory of her."*
>
> —Matthew 26:6–13

Broken

Grief and Love Poured Out

In spite of the fact that Jesus said He was going to die in Jerusalem, every one of His friends was telling Him that He wasn't. All except one.

Only Mary of Bethany accepted the sorrow. Only she believed . . . and grieved what He said was going to happen. And only she seemed to realize that these were their last precious moments with Jesus.

Just days before the cross, Simon the former leper threw a dinner party and invited Jesus and His disciples and friends. Over the roar of chatter and clatter, Jesus's thoughts must have hung, suspended and heavy. He would soon come face-to-face with the evil of sin. He would soon face the cross. The weight of that reality must have felt ominous and tangible to Him, despite the party laughter. Into this scene, walked Mary.

She knew the time was short. In spite of the others' denial of Jesus's upcoming suffering, Mary drew alongside Him. She alone encouraged Him as He obeyed His Father.

With her life-savings represented in the alabaster jar of perfume, Mary broke the bottle's neck and poured the oil over Jesus's head, down His body, over His feet, as if embalming Him. The symbolism was not lost on Jesus. He understood she was preparing Him for burial.

Mary had developed the habit of breaking cultural rules. First, she had sat at Jesus's feet when He was a guest in her home, something no respectable woman would do. It angered her sister, Martha, but it pleased the Lord. Now, as she poured out this exquisite oil, she incensed the disciples, but again, she pleased the Lord.

"Let her alone." Jesus had defended her. "She has just done something significant and wonderful for me." (See Matthew 26:10.)

And that was her only intent. She did what she could to bless Him. She could not stop the evil that waited to envelop Him, but she could express this tenderness for Him while He was still with them. Her tears communicated her sorrow. Her sacrifice made it clear she knew His death was near.

So potent was the perfume that Mary emptied out that it would have clung to Jesus's hair and skin for days. Perhaps it was the one trace of comfort for Jesus to smell its lingering aroma as He suffered and sweat and bled through those extensive hours of torture and dying. The sweet fragrance was the memory of grief and love poured out—as He did the same. BP

Who Could Love Them More?

Rescue a struggling caterpillar too early from its cocoon, and it won't have developed the strength to survive as a butterfly. Release a foolish child too early from consequences, and he or she won't have the wisdom to deal with the bigger issues of life. Ignore or offer false forgiveness for an offense against you, and your loved one won't see his or her need for repentance and forgiveness from God.

A wise friend lets God be God in her loved ones' lives. A wise parent knows that growth is a process. Short-circuit the process, and the lesson will be lost.

Some call it tough love. But it's really tenderness personified.

Sometimes the most loving expression of commitment is to simply come alongside someone you love who's hurting, be quiet, and let God do the work only He can. Real love entrusts to God what you know you can't help or heal.

Contrary to how that might feel—like you're setting that person out to drift—remember that you were never a good life-preserver to begin with. You want your loved one to experience the only long-term, real search-and-rescue effort there is. That's always been Jesus's mission, and never yours. As great as your love is for your friend, your child, your parent—God loves him or her more. As deep as your insight is into that person's character, God's is deeper. You can go the distance, but God goes further. You can only see today. God sees that person's completion.

And He's not finished. He's committed to making His children like His Son. He's building a relationship with your loved one that has a bigger goal in mind than just relief from today's crisis.

Even God, seeing His sinless Son take on all the weight and waste of the world, didn't rescue Him from the cross. There was something bigger going on. (BP)

We cannot be an encouragement if we live our lives in secret caves, pushing people away from us. People out of touch don't encourage others. Encouragement is a face-to-face thing.

—Chuck Swindoll

ON A MISSION

What positive rescue missions have you attempted?

- A stray cat or dog or other animal?
- A struggling swimmer?
- Someone from a burning building?
- A stranger with no change at a parking meter or tollbooth?
- A trapped bird inside your house?
- A lost file on a computer?
- A girlfriend from a bad blind date?

Mary's perfume, nard, is a fragrant oil made from the spikenard plant grown in northern India. The amount that Mary used, one pound, was worth a year's wage. This perfume was most likely Mary's dowry.

Jesus & Martha of Bethany

> *Martha . . . when she heard that Jesus was coming, went to meet Him. . . . Martha then said to Jesus, "Lord, if You had been here, my brother would not have died." . . . Jesus said to her, "Your brother will rise again. . . . I am the resurrection and the life; he who believes in Me will live even if he dies, and everyone who lives and believes in Me will never die. Do you believe this?"*
>
> —*John 11:20–21, 23, 25–26*

Disillusioned

Learning the Lesson of Faith

The setting was in the little hamlet of Bethany, inside the home of Lazarus and his sisters, Martha and Mary. It was the place where Jesus often found rest and refreshment when surrounded by the pressures of responsibilities. He unwound in Bethany. In this little home he was not faced with a constant barrage of questions or the push for another miracle. He was among friends.

Lazarus was not one of the twelve disciples, but he was just as loved by the Lord. So when Lazarus fell ill and his sisters sent a message to Jesus, they were certain He would come quickly. But He didn't. In fact, He purposefully delayed going . . . for two days!

When Martha heard that Jesus was finally nearby, she left the house and ran down the path to meet Jesus en route. Seeing Him on the road, Martha stood before Jesus and said, "Lord, if You had been here, my brother would not have died. Even now I know that whatever You ask of God, God will give You" (John 11:21–22). It's as if she said, "Look, God will give it to You, but He didn't give it to us. My brother's in the tomb, Lord. He's been there four days. Where in the world were You?"

Jesus's loving response is terribly moving. It's not a rebuke but a promise. Perhaps Jesus took her head in His hands and held it closely. Or maybe He put his arms around her and embraced her as He said softly to Martha, whom He did love, "Martha . . ." And, with the words almost under His breath: "I am the resurrection and the life; he who believes in Me will live even if he dies, and everyone who lives and believes in Me will never die. Do you believe this?" (11:25–26).

The Lord understands our times of disillusionment—those times when we ask Him to bring life where there is death but He delays. The Lord wants to hear our honest feelings, especially during times of deep sorrow. He never rebukes tears shed in faith. He only asks us to believe that He is who He said He is: the resurrection and the life.

—*Charles R. Swindoll*

The divine perspective says, "Lord, I'm facing a crisis. But I know I can trust You; I want to trust You. Lord, I submit. I resign myself to Your plan. And with great delight, I wait upon Your answer."

—Chuck Swindoll

When God Feels FAR AWAY

Sooner or later, we all will grieve.

As much as anything else, loss is part of life. Grieving reminds us that someone is missing. As painful as it is, we can persevere through just about anything as long as we sense that God is with us. But our courage melts when that missing person in our lives is God.

God's silence is one of the most confusing experiences a Christ-follower can endure. It's in God's silence that we must come back to what it means to live by faith.

Do I believe God is with me even as I stand alone at this fresh grave? How about six months later when the well-wishers are gone?

Do I believe God has my best interests at heart even when I don't sense His presence?

In times of grief, we often feel like we're just going through the motions. We have faith to believe God is at work but sometimes it seems like He's at work everywhere but within us. We may even feel embarrassed in front of our church friends or want to avoid them because our faith seems hollow.

But contrary to what we may think, this is familiar territory for God's people. Because we all feel lost sometimes.

The prophet Isaiah called Jesus the "man of sorrows" for good reason (Isaiah 53:3). Jesus never lived far from grief. John 11 gives us a front-row seat to witness Jesus in His very personal moments of grief at the loss of His close friend Lazarus. That scene alone convinces us that Jesus knows what it feels like to grieve.

With the same compassion He extended to Martha, Jesus Himself prays for you today. Hebrews 7:25 makes this amazing statement: "Therefore He is able also to save forever those who draw near to God through Him, since He always lives to make intercession for them." Jesus lives to intercede for you. Before you ever kneel down to pour out your heart to God, Jesus Christ has already called out to His Father on your behalf. Even before you ask, Jesus knows firsthand what you need—because He's *with* you.

You will at times feel as though God is far away, but don't you believe it. He is *with* you. Start by trusting that truth.

That reality may not remove the struggle of the grieving process, but it will help. When you believe that God is there—a very present help *in* trouble—when you reach out to Him in the darkness, you will find comfort.

God is *with* you. BP

TELLING ALL

Tell God all that is in your heart, as one unloads one's heart, its pleasures and its pains, to a dear friend.

Tell Him your troubles, that He may comfort you;

tell Him your joys, that He may sober them;

tell Him your longings, that He may purify them;

tell Him your dislikes, that He may help you conquer them;

talk to Him of your temptations, that He may shield you from them:

show Him the wounds of your heart, that He may heal them. . . .

If you thus pour out all your weaknesses, needs, troubles, there will be no lack of what to say. . . . Talk out of the abundance of the heart, without consideration . . . say just what [you] think. Blessed are they who attain to such familiar, unreserved intercourse with God.

—Francois Fenelon (1651–1715)[7]

The tradition of saving tears in a bottle has endured for more than three thousand years. Based on Psalm 56:8, when David said that God saved his tears in a bottle, tear bottles—or lachrymatory—were common in ancient Middle Eastern societies. Mourners filled small glass vials with tears and placed them in burial tombs as symbols of their love and respect.

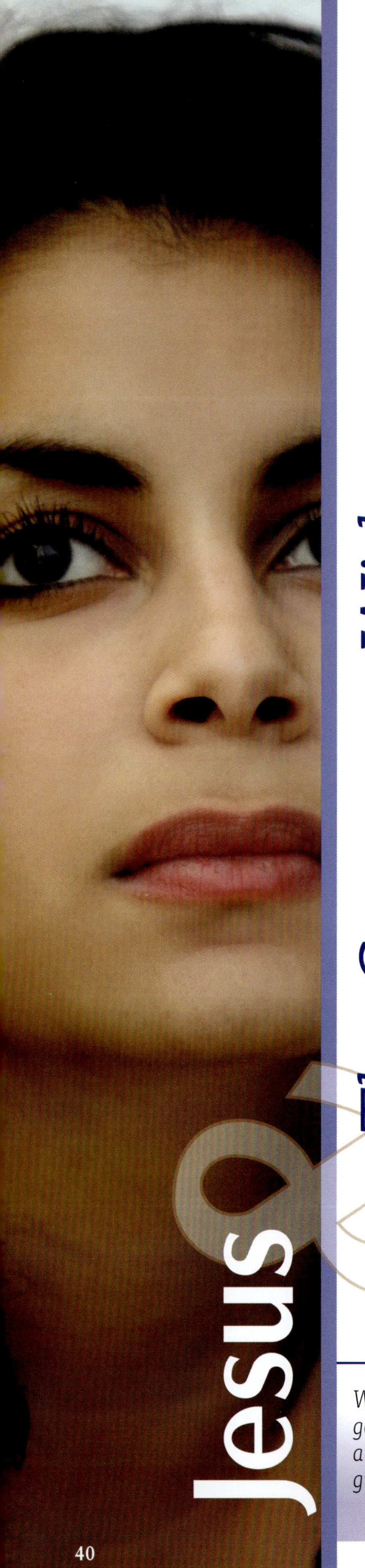

> *"Truly I say to you, this poor widow put in more than all the contributors to the treasury; for they all put in out of their surplus, but she, out of her poverty, put in all she owned, all she had to live on."*
>
> —*Mark 12:43–44*

Jesus & The Generous Widow

Wholehearted

Piety Despite Poverty

Jesus had just blasted the religious leaders for their blatant hypocrisy. He punctuated His condemnation of their pretense with a promise never to enter the temple again until they learned to say of Him, "Blessed is He who comes in the name of the Lord!" (Matthew 23:39).

On His way out of the temple, Jesus sat down in the Court of the Women and observed those who made donations to the treasury. To be sure, this seemed an odd place to pause, but the Lord had a lesson to teach His disciples.

A number of offering boxes sat in the temple to collect freewill offerings.[8] Jesus observed as rich people threw in large sums of money. He also noted a poor widow who "put in two small copper coins, which amount to a cent" (Mark 12:42). The King James Version translates the word for "coins" as "mites," a term derived from the French, *miete*, signifying a crumb or a tiny morsel.[9] These coins represented the smallest and least valuable currency in Israel. Practically speaking, the widow's donation was worth next to nothing.

Jesus called His disciples over and uttered these startling words: "Truly I say to you, this poor widow put in more than all the contributors to the treasury; for they all put in out of their surplus, but she, out of her poverty, put in all she owned, all she had to live on" (12:43–44).

Jesus revealed that God values the heart far more than the amount given. Most people contributed "out of their surplus"—from what they didn't need. But the widow gave sacrificially—"out of her poverty"—donating everything as a non-compulsory, freewill offering! This revealed her heart, that her complete trust was in the Lord. She was the kind of person whom Paul later wrote about: "Now she who is a widow indeed and who has been left alone, has fixed her hope on God and continues in entreaties and prayers night and day" (1 Timothy 5:5). This generous widow stood in stark contrast to the religious leaders Jesus had just blasted—those who did good deeds only "for appearance's sake" (Mark 12:40).

Jesus still watches the treasury. He weighs the value of the heart that contributes rather than the amount contributed (2 Corinthians 8:12). The widow remains a model for us, not that we should adopt a vow of poverty but that we should be poor in spirit, humble, self-sacrificing, and totally dependent on God—regardless our financial status. WS

We become increasingly more aware of God's blessings as we reflect upon them. In His goodness, He gives us the gift of life, deliverance from sin, and protection in a hostile and angry world. That alone should keep us busy lifting our hearts in praise, adoration, and gratitude to the Lord!

—*Chuck Swindoll*

Generosity from a HEART STIRRED

Some of the poorest people you will ever meet are extremely generous. And some of the richest people you will know are tight-fisted. How much one has makes virtually no impact on how much one gives.

Have you noticed that receiving a lot doesn't make you more openhanded? You might be grateful at times, but that doesn't make you generous. Sometimes all it does is spoil you.

Only your heart determines the difference. Generosity and a heart inclined go hand in hand. Facts and figures on how great the need is are important, but they never make you generous. Sensible reasoning and sound logic offer helpful information, but you never dig as deeply as you do when your heart is stirred from deep within.

When God told His people to build a place of worship in the desert, He compelled them to pull out all the stops. Exodus 25 begins God's detailed description of what He wanted the tabernacle to look like—and who should build it. God had one condition for those who got to play a part: "every man whose heart moves him" (Exodus 25:2). God didn't want reluctant givers. No grudging gifts. The New Testament echoes this same requirement: "God loves a cheerful giver" (2 Corinthians 9:7).

Do you wonder why your heart is not stirred like this more often?

The answer can be found, in part, in Exodus 31:12–15. Your heart is stirred when you rest and reflect on your relationship with the Lord. Your heart isn't stirred in the fast lane. Generosity takes intent. You need a period of time to be quiet. Put the to-do list aside. Get alone. Turn your thoughts toward the greatness of God in your life. Ask Him if you can participate in something for Him that will bring Him glory—some act of ministry in His name. Mind you, God doesn't need it, but you need to do it. Make your gift something special that you offer to Him.

When you get involved personally in a project for the greater glory of God—something that's bigger than you and bigger than you could ever imagine—your heart will be stirred to generosity.

You are never more like God than when you give—without recognition, without reservation, without reluctance, without restriction. There's good reason why "charity" also means love.

—*Charles R. Swindoll*

Get JOY

Four Ways to Add Joy to Your Giving

1. Reflect on God's gifts to you. Hasn't He been good? Better than we deserve (as Dave Ramsey always says). Sufficient food, clothing, and safe shelters. Even more blessings of good health, happy families, and close friends . . . and so much more.

2. Remind yourself of His promises regarding generosity. Call to mind a few biblical principles that promise the benefits of sowing bountifully. Spiritual bumper crops . . . are God's specialty.

3. Examine your heart. Nobody but you can do this. Open that private vault and ask several hard questions, like:

- Is my giving proportionate to my income?
- Am I motivated by guilt . . . or by contagious joy?
- If someone else knew the level of my giving to God's work, would I be a model to follow?
- Have I prayed about and made a plan for giving . . . or am I an impulsive responder?

4. Trust God to honor consistent generosity. Here's the big step, but it's essential. Go for it! When you really believe God is leading you to make a significant contribution—release your restraint and develop the habit of generosity.[10]

—Charles R. Swindoll

Copper coins changed hands in the marketplace of Jesus's day as quickly and easily as pennies are exchanged today. The Jewish and Roman coins pictured here represent the clash between the culture and conviction. Roman money pictured Caesar and pagan religious symbols, while Jewish currency illustrated nature.

Faith Served Daily

Ney Bailey

Insight for Living board of directors member Ney has invested her life in the ministry of Campus Crusade for Christ International, speaking and sharing about the love and grace of God with students and staff all over the world for five decades. If you could sit with Ney over coffee, you'd hear amazing accounts of God's faithfulness in her life story—from the twenty years she ministered in Eastern Europe behind the Iron Curtain, to the circumstances that led to her helping to initiate Crusade's Family Life Conference and Ministry. Ney could also give firsthand witness to how God has been faithful to Insight for Living as she's served on our leadership board since 1980.

What's One Prayer You Say Often?

"Before I go into new situations or meet new people, I say, *Lord, I pray that I can be to them what they need in You, and only You know what that is.*"

On Being a Woman

"I love that Jesus broke all cultural barriers to love and value women. It was to a woman He first appeared after His resurrection and to a woman He first gave the call to tell others that He had risen. He loved and valued women, and they loved Him in return. I am grateful to be one of them."

What's Always in Your Fridge?

"Dog food."*

*Cynthia Swindoll recalls a birthday when Bailey, Ney's cockapoo, sang "Happy Birthday" to Cynthia over the phone.

On Faith and Feelings

"We're so prone to listen to our feelings and our circumstances. But we can use them as a springboard to take us to God's Word. Faith is *not* a feeling; it's a *choice* we have to take God at His word."*

*See more about Ney's best-selling book *Faith Is Not a Feeling* on page 57.

Why Are You on the Insight for Living Board of Directors?

"Chuck's teaching of the Word of God in a practical, up-to-date, relevant, sometimes humorous way reaches people for Christ and makes disciples all over the world. I love being a part of this mission!"

One of Ney's Favorite Verses

For the Lord God is a sun and shield;
The Lord gives grace and glory;
No good thing does He withhold from those
who walk uprightly. —Psalm 84:11

Jesus & The Woman Healed on the Sabbath

And He was teaching in one of the synagogues on the Sabbath. And there was a woman who for eighteen years had had a sickness caused by a spirit; and she was bent double, and could not straighten up at all. When Jesus saw her, He called her over and said to her, "Woman, you are freed from your sickness." And He laid His hands on her; and immediately she was made erect again and began glorifying God.

—Luke 13:10–13

Released

Restored to Full Height

Jesus had crossed the line. While the Pharisees found no violation in rescuing an ox or a donkey from a well on the Sabbath, they thought it was just too much work to release a twisted woman from nearly two decades of deformity on the Sabbath.

And Jesus pushed back. Almost as if to say, *Are you kidding me? You just witnessed a miracle, yet you sit in judgment because of what day of the week it is?*

Jesus knew all too well what day it was. He may have even intentionally chosen the Sabbath for this miracle so the Pharisees' outrageous, offensive hypocrisy would be brought to the surface. He may have even specially chosen a Sabbath to rescue that dear one who had suffered so long at Satan's hand. She was certainly deemed the lowliest in the synagogue—an older woman, deformed at that. Hardly worth the Pharisees' attention.

Truth was, they probably had never once noticed the contorted woman. Mercifully, she wasn't able to see the scorn in their eyes. It had been years since she had looked into anyone's eyes. From her demon-inflicted bow, face-down toward the dirt, she saw only their feet. Like someone born blind, she knew the world by their voices.

When the mysterious, strong voice echoed across the synagogue and called her out of the shadows, she was as shocked as the Pharisees. Why would someone notice her? Or call her to the front of the synagogue? Scandalous! She had so long been prey to the enemy that she hardly knew what to do. She moved toward this shepherd, come to rescue her from the spiritual wolves devouring her soul. The Pharisees were wagging their fingers at the grace so blatantly lavished on this Sabbath. Jesus knew He was "breaking the rules."

Jesus asked her nothing about her faith or the condition of her heart. He had another lesson and audience in mind. But He did call her "woman" in the same honorable way He would have addressed His mother. And He restored her to her full height—in body and spirit. BP

Loving God, thank you for accepting me and forgiving me when I was lost, afraid, confused, and so far away from You. I am thankful that You heard my prayer and took me seriously, even though I did not know how to express my faith in Jesus very well. All I knew to do was to come as a little child, and You graciously took me in. Thank You for making it possible to know eternal life with You — today.

—Chuck Swindoll

Down to GRACE

The Puritans called the Sabbath "the market day of the soul." While on other days our attention is spent in the marketplace, on this day we are to do business with God.

The Sabbath is a day considered holy or "set apart" from the norm. God established the Sabbath so we might rest from life's busyness and find restoration in worshiping Him. A Sabbath stillness reminds us that God is God—and we are not. It takes us back to basics.

You look at things differently when you're not distracted by life's noise. A time of stillness will often take away all other crutches and leave you with nothing but God. You're "down to grace" alone. And in the quiet, you may hear God say, *This is a very good place to be.*

Determine to set aside time for a regular Sabbath rest—a time for solitude and connection with God. Maybe even cancel something . . . and resist the urge to fill that time. Allow the words of Psalm 46:10 to flood your mind: "Be still, and know that I am God" (NIV).

Before your "Sabbath" is over, be it a day or an hour, pray for those in trouble who have not yet realized the Savior's offer of rescue. For those weary of fighting for their marriages. For those in despair who are planning to end their lives. Stand in their place and ask God to bring them to faith.

Also acknowledge to God that you have problems, and know that it's up to Him to solve them. Tell God about your heartaches and that you are relying on His grace to heal them. Tell him about your material needs and that you are counting on His provision to meet them. Then, just listen. Stop, be still, and listen.

What you discover in the Sabbath rest is that God sees you. You may feel invisible; you may think your need is unknown—or at least unimportant to God. But nothing is further from the truth. He's not missing a single detail in your life. He hears your conversations. He sees your checkbook. He knows your unspoken fears. He's watching the depth of the water and the temperature of the furnace. He's pouring out the strength you need to endure in the minute you feel you can't go on.

At this moment, God is watching your life, and during Sabbath times of stillness, He shows you He is enough. BP

What Every Woman Should KNOW HOW TO DO

Drive a stick shift and jump a car battery

Break up, apologize, and forgive

Take Scripture to heart

Create something beautiful with her hands (such as a meal, a comfortable home, a handmade gift)

Interview well

Use a fire extinguisher

Sew a button or a hem

Move gracefully and joyfully through the seasons of life

What's the big deal about the Sabbath?

When God instituted the Sabbath, His intent was to have special access to His children's hearts on that day. It has never been about particular activities to refrain from—it's always been about hearts being open to God's presence.

When Jesus saw that the disciples were overwrought by their hectic pace, He called them apart. He didn't just say, "Get away from everything"; instead, He called them away. The purpose of the time set apart was to be with Him and be restored. (See Mark 6:31.)

Jesus & Mrs. Zebedee (the Mother of James and John)

Then the mother of the sons of Zebedee came to Jesus with her sons, bowing down and making a request of Him. And He said to her, "What do you wish?" She said to Him, "Command that in Your kingdom these two sons of mine may sit one on Your right and one on Your left." . . . And hearing this, the ten became indignant with the two brothers. But Jesus called them to Himself and said, "You know that the rulers of the Gentiles lord it over them, and their great men exercise authority over them. It is not this way among you, but whoever wishes to become great among you shall be your servant."

—*Matthew 20:20–21, 24–26*

Servanthood

The Flip Side of Leadership

It's a mother's job to be proud of her kids. What young boy hasn't rolled his eyes at his mother going on about him? It's embarrassing (but secretly heartwarming). So we can't be terribly hard on "Mrs. Zebedee," the wife of a Galilean fisherman and doting mother of disciples James and John.

Her motive was probably pure. She didn't ask that her sons occupy the center throne; of course not—that belongs to Jesus. But she did nominate James and John as candidates for thrones number two and number three—one on Jesus's right and the other on His left. After all, her boys left their nets and entered Jesus's up-and-coming ministry. They were among the first He called to be a part of "the Twelve" and that needed recognition!

It's easy to commiserate with the other ten disciples about James and John sending their mom to pull strings with Jesus. They were angry. No doubt a bit jealous. No way were they going to give up those top spots without a fight.

Sadly, all of them missed the point.

Jesus must have felt quite alone watching His entire troupe jockeying for position after He had modeled in such sharp contrast what godly leadership looked like. The cutthroat corporate ladder was not the model. And it wasn't like ranks in the military. Nor like top athletes on a team. "It's not going to be that way with you," He must have sighed.

Jesus pulled them aside and taught them in low tones about the "great reversal" principle of leadership: whoever wants to be great must become a servant. The setting of this classroom spoke volumes. They were on their way to Jerusalem, together for the last time.

"I came to serve, not be served," He told them, "and to give My life away." (See Matthew 20:28.)

His words later haunted them. When the soldiers hammered Jesus's hands to the rough wood of the cross—one on the left and the other on the right—the disciples saw personified the picture of servant leadership.

Finally . . . they got it.[11]

—*Charles R. Swindoll*

"Whoever wishes to become great among you shall be your servant" (Matthew 20:26). Forgotten words . . . even in many of our churches we get so caught up in a success and size race that we lose sight of our primary calling as followers of Christ: stand back and be a servant.

—Chuck Swindoll

True **Submission**

The "me before you" attitude gets us in trouble every time. What makes it especially challenging is how natural and easy it is for us to think this way. What's hard for us is to say, "You're in charge of me." Our natural predisposition is to resist authority on all levels. We like things equal. We like to have our say. When we don't, our pride gets hurt . . . which in the long run is a very good thing.

Think about it—every good step you've made in your spiritual life has been a step of humility, and every step of pride has been a step backward.

Humility stands empty-handed before God. No demands, no requests. All you can do is submit yourself to God, then submit yourself to what God has allowed, acknowledging that He's got a bigger purpose in mind than today's issues.

Whatever brings pressure to our lives—a stressful job, a difficult marriage, a chronic illness, a financial crisis—God uses to reveal pride and prompt humility. Too often our choice is to resist and resent that prompt or give in to despair. But we can choose to say, "You before me, Lord. Do whatever You think is best. What do You want to teach me?" God loves a moment like that! In the furnace of that God-designed challenge He exposes our need and bring us to the end of ourselves: He shapes our characters.

While He stiff-arms the arrogant, the self-promoter, and the self-sufficient, He pours grace on the humble. He runs to their rescue. He offers Himself in exchange for our surrendered rights to our lives.

We want to manage our own lives. But we also want to live in the blessings of God. The only way to do that is to choose to humble ourselves under God's hand and say,

> I relinquish my rights and expectations to control my life and humbly ask God by His grace to replace these with a grateful spirit for whatever in His wisdom He chooses to allow for my life. I believe that His will is my ultimate good, and I want above everything else to bring Him glory. (BP)

Your Deepest Longing **Filled**

It is God who loved us first, His unceasing love sends Him after us. He is the seeking Lover, the One who has made us for Himself. From the very beginning, we were created to be found and loved by Him. He has woven this secret into the very fibers of our soul. When we seek Him with all the longing He has placed in our hearts, in the end, we simply discover Him seeking us, loving us in all times and in all places.

—author unknown

Bible Insight

John and James's mother asked Jesus to credit her sons with the coveted right and left positions to the throne. Scripture repeatedly talks about Jesus being at the Father's "right hand" (Acts 2:33; 5:31; 7:55; Romans 8:34; Colossians 3:1). This position speaks of authority, honor, and glory. This proud mother wanted these tributes for her two boys. Jesus told her she didn't have a clue what she was asking for.

Jesus & The Woman Giving Blessing

"Blessed is the womb that bore You and the breasts at which You nursed." But [Jesus] said, "On the contrary, blessed are those who hear the word of God and observe it."

—Luke 11:27–28

Blessedness

Obedience to God's Word

"Amen!"

A lone voice cried out from the crowd. "How blessed Your mother is—the one who gave You birth and nourished You at her breast. What a great blessing You are, and the mother who brought You forth!"

It was a startling thing to say at that moment. Jesus hadn't been talking about family but about demons and humans (Luke 11:14–26). Why then this sudden blessing on His mother? Perhaps it broke the tension—Jesus had just been accused of driving out demons by the power of the Prince of Demons. Or maybe it offered a note of encouragement, assurance that someone in the crowd agreed with His message. We may never know for sure, but whatever the purpose, the blessing was startling—not just because of the timing but because it came from the voice of a woman.

It was a brave thing to do—to interrupt a rabbi—in a crowd filled with men. Yet this woman was compelled to express her gratitude for Jesus's ministry by blessing His mother—for nurturing a Son who was and still is a source of blessing to the nations.

Jesus didn't rebuke this woman; He affirmed her. He taught her that real blessing doesn't come from family relationships but from the spiritual relationships we can have with God as His obedient children. Before Jesus's lecture to the crowd about demons, He had told an inquisitive lawyer the parable of the Good Samaritan (10:25–37). Jesus had also pointed out His friend Mary's devotion on a visit He had paid to her and her sister, Martha, in Bethany (10:38–42), and He had instructed His disciples in how to pray (11:1–13). These three encounters serve as illustrations of Jesus's teaching about blessedness and obedience. How blessed are those who obey the Word by caring for others, by making Jesus the focal point of their lives, and by humbling themselves before God in prayer.

Blessed be the womb and breast of the mother of Jesus—yes. But twice blessed be the one who obeys Jesus's voice. (DJ)

The longer you walk in a seasoned spirit with the Lord, the easier you ought to be to live with. You think before you speak. You trust the living Lord to settle you deep within, to give you the controls that you need emotionally, to give you a discerning mind so that you see evil even when it's masked—and to help your children see it.

—Chuck Swindoll

A New Reason to Celebrate MOTHER'S DAY

Tradition teaches us to wear flowers on Mother's Day to honor our mothers: red if she is living, white if she has passed away. Also on that day in May, churches often honor mothers in the congregation by asking them to stand and by giving them lovely flowers to represent love and gratitude. Local florists are never busier than on this one day!

But Mother's Day holds a mixed bouquet of emotions.

For some of us, memories of our relationships with our moms are not the sweetest—or perhaps our children could say the same. If we wrap our identities around either side of that equation, we're in for trouble.

For others of us, when half the congregation stands to receive their flowers on that dreaded Sunday morning, we remain seated—with arms and hearts empty. For whatever reason, this longed-for gift from God hasn't been given to us, and in that moment, the seeming unfairness weighs heavily.

We know of a couple opportunities Jesus had to memorialize Mother's Day. On one occasion when He was preaching, a woman in the crowd blurted out a blessing on His mother—a perfect "Hallmark moment" for Jesus to honor His own mother. But instead, Jesus pointed to another reason for celebration. "Blessed are those who hear the word of God and observe it" (Luke 11:28).

In that one statement, Jesus redefined our reasons to honor women and changed everything for all of us.

The role of motherhood is a gift from God—a high responsibility of influence, and for many, the best opportunity to picture God's love and care to a generation. But every woman, whether by biology or example, has the responsibility to be fruitful and multiply by advancing God's purposes in others' lives. What may be physically out of reach for some can be redeemed by us all by living and breathing God's Word in our circles of influence.

Who you are in Christ is not determined by a role you play in your life. Neither are you the sum total of what others say about you—well-meaning or just mean. You are who God says you are. You are His. You have been bought back for the purpose of showing the world Christ. You are rescued, forgiven, and loved. Blessed are you, God says, when you live like it.

Hold the bouquet high, ladies—you belong to Jesus. 

Remember Who You Are

I Am His . . .

Beloved—Song of Solomon 2:16

Letter—2 Corinthians 3:2

Child—1 John 3:17

Delight—Zephaniah 3:17

Workmanship—Ephesians 2:10

He Is My . . .

Shepherd—Psalm 23:1

Fortress—Psalm 18:2

Helper—John 14:16–17

Life—Colossians 3:4

Light—Psalm 27:1

Being a mother was a woman's highest ambition in Bible times. Her future, as well as her family's future, depended on it. As much as motherhood was seen as a blessing from God, in that culture not being able to conceive (for any reason) was considered God's curse. Dozens of times in Scripture we see God using a season of waiting for a baby as the means to test a woman's faith.

Walking a Real Road

Kristy

Listener Ministries representative Kristy connects with wonderful people from all over the country every day on the phone. She loves to hear how God is using His Word taught on the *Insight for Living* broadcast to touch people right where they live. She also loves a good recipe now and then to feed her favorite men: her husband, Brett, and son, Nathan.

A Memorable Connection on the Phones

"I prayed with a caller one day who then asked me how she could pray for me. Before the call ended, she lifted my needs to the Lord. Wow—isn't that great?"

An Everyday Miracle

"God uses us even when we don't know we're being used. Just put aside selfish desires and serve. Love at all times—you just don't know all the ways He's working."

On Walking together in Friendship

"This year 'the Scrappin Sisters,' six of my scrapbooking buddies and I, walked more than five hundred miles to train for the Susan G. Komen 3-Day for the Cure sixty-mile walk-a-thon. We participated on behalf of one of our 'sisters' who has breast cancer. It was a true blessing! We all benefited from the wonderful experience—including the great stress relief, fellowship, and prayer time we enjoyed."

A Lesson Learned so Far

"Life is hard, but trusting in Him is worth it all! Even when we think we know what's best, His way is always better."

One of Kristy's Favorite Verses

Search me, O God, and know my heart;
Try me and know my anxious thoughts;
And see if there be any hurtful way in me,
And lead me in the everlasting way. —Psalm 139:23–24

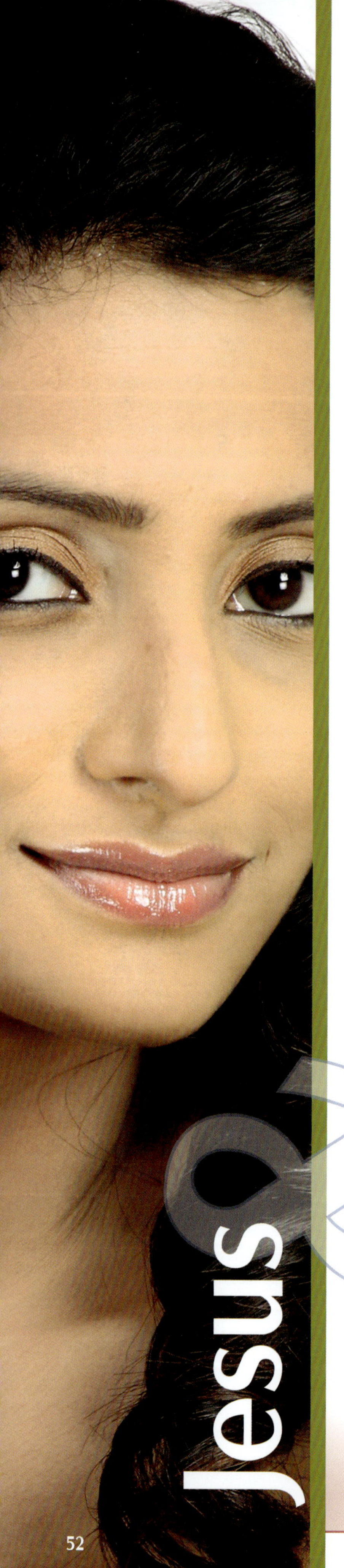

> *While [Pilate] was sitting on the judgment seat, his wife sent him a message, saying, "Have nothing to do with that righteous Man; for last night I suffered greatly in a dream because of Him."*
>
> *—Matthew 27:19*

Caution

A Well-Timed Warning

Dark shadows had fallen over Jerusalem.

A lone figure knelt, weeping, agonizing in prayer, as eleven men slumbered nearby. While Jerusalem slept, the Lord Jesus endured anguish in the darkness of Gethsemane. But He did not suffer alone that night.

On the other side of Jerusalem in the luxuriant palace of the governor—perhaps even during the hours of Jesus's agony in the garden—another figure writhed in agony. Whatever the content of her nightmare concerning Christ, it caused her to arrive at a firm conclusion: His innocence.

Twelve years earlier, the Roman Senate had debated a proposal that no wife could accompany a provincial magistrate in his duty.[12] Had that proposition passed, Pontius Pilate's wife would not have been present at this critical historical juncture.

Tradition records her name as Claudia Procula, and some churches even consider her a saint.[13] Although we have no evidence that she converted to Christianity, it is fascinating that the five other dreams recorded in Matthew were divinely inspired to those who worshiped God—and several of the dreams served as warnings.

After conducting three illegal trials that night, the religious leaders dragged Jesus to the Praetorium, the residence of Pontius Pilate and his wife. Following an initial examination, Pilate told the Jews he found no guilt in Jesus (John 18:38). Pilate then passed Jesus off to Herod Antipas for judgment, but Herod returned the prisoner with an implication of Jesus's innocence (Luke 23:13–15). Sitting on his official judgment seat, Pilate gave the crowds the choice of which prisoner he would release to freedom—Jesus or the notorious Barabbas.

Just then, Pilate's wife sent him the message: "Have nothing to do with that righteous Man; for last night I suffered greatly in a dream because of Him" (Matthew 27:19). What timing! God affirmed the innocence of Jesus a number of times by Pilate's own mouth. Now his wife punctuated that verdict as her message reached him—and while he sat on his official judgment seat!

The Gospels make it plain that Pilate recognized Jesus's blamelessness. But for fear of jeopardizing his political favor—both with Rome and with the people—Pilate chose the more expedient route and condemned Christ to death.

Pilate flattened every fence erected to vindicate the innocence of Jesus—including the unusual nightmare and well-timed warning from his wife.

How foolish.

God often validates His will for our lives through a number of providentially planned circumstances. A well-timed word . . . a surprising verdict . . . an unusual dream . . . the words of a spouse—these frequently work in concert with Scripture (never in contradiction) to affirm the truth that we should follow. WS

DISCERNMENT

D*iscernment:* the skill and accuracy to read character. The ability to detect and identify the real truth. To see beneath the surface and correctly "size up" the situation. To read between the lines of the visible . . . the obvious.

Is discernment a valuable trait? See what God says and then answer for yourself . . .

God gave Solomon "an understanding heart to judge [God's] people [and] to discern between good and evil" (1 Kings 3:9). The apostle Paul informed us that discernment accompanies genuine spirituality (1 Corinthians 2:14–16). Hebrews 5:14 calls it a mark of maturity.

Discernment gives us a proper frame of reference, a definite line separating good and evil. It acts as an umpire in life and blows the whistle on the fakes. Discernment picks and chooses its dates with great care. It doesn't fall for fakes, flirt with phonies, or dance with deceivers. Discernment learns how to distinguish the fools from the children and the sleeping from the wise.

Discernment says, "Stop believing everything you hear. Quit being so easily convinced. Be selective. Think!"

Want discernment but don't know where to find it?

Go to your *knees*. James 1:5 promises wisdom to those who ask for it.

Go to the *Word*. Psalm 119:98–100 offers insight beyond your fondest dreams.

Go to the *wise*. Discernment is better caught than taught. Those who have this rare disease are often highly contagious.

God offers discernment to those who are willing. It's an offer that's good throughout life and comes with a satisfaction-guaranteed clause. All may apply, even those who think they know it all, and know not that they know nothing.[14]

—Charles R. Swindoll

A Discerner's Test
Four Kinds of People

He who knows not, and knows not that he knows not, is a fool, shun him;

He who knows not, and knows that he knows not, is a child, teach him;

He who knows, and knows not that he knows, is asleep, wake him;

He who knows, and knows that he knows, is wise, follow him.

—Persian proverb[15]

What comes from the Lord because it is impossible for humans to manufacture it? Wisdom. What brings wisdom and dispels worry? Worship. Let nothing detract from your time of personal worship today. Let nothing frighten you . . . nothing from yesterday's past, today's present, or tomorrow's future. Nothing.

—Chuck Swindoll

The Citadel dominates the walls along the western side of Jerusalem's Old City today. Herod the Great built the bastion as his palace, a residence so ornate that the Jewish historian Josephus wrote, "[It] exceeds all my ability to describe it."[16] The king's extensive palace stretched from today's Jaffa Gate almost the entire length of the Armenian Quarter. From the time the Romans began to govern Israel in AD 6, the Roman governor, or procurator, resided in the lavish palace whenever he visited Jerusalem. Because Pontius Pilate stayed at the palace, or Praetorium, he probably judged Jesus here rather than at the Antonia Fortress, as some believe (a common misconception whose tradition is hard to uproot; see Mark 15:16; John 18:28).[17]

Jesus & The Women Disciples

Soon afterwards, He began going around from one city and village to another, proclaiming and preaching the kingdom of God. The twelve were with Him, and also some women who had been healed of evil spirits and sicknesses: Mary who was called Magdalene, from whom seven demons had gone out, and Joanna the wife of Chuza, Herod's steward, and Susanna, and many others who were contributing to their support out of their private means.

—*Luke 8:1–3*

Devoted

Support from Behind the Scenes

One of the mysteries of Jesus's ministry is money. Where did it come from? Who paid for travel, food, and lodging for twelve men for three years? No one took an offering or asked for funds. Jesus got no honorarium for His unscheduled speaking engagements.

Funding came from an unexpected source. Much of Jesus's cause was sustained by women who poured out their own money like precious oil to enable Jesus to teach and train, moving up and down the countryside at His Father's wishes.

They were not Jesus's "groupies," though no doubt their intentions were often misread. These generous women were genuine disciples who followed, served, listened, and obeyed. And while the typical disciple around Jesus was "called," these women just came.

Of the many, only a few had their names recorded—Joanna from Herod's high society, Susanna, Mary, James's mother, and Mary Magdalene (the only one who had anything she said recorded in Scripture). Yet how many times were these women in the room while Jesus taught—tending to details or serving the meal? In typical fashion, Jesus would not have shooed them off like other rabbis of the day or dismissed them when He and the men sat up late talking by the fire. What stories these women could have told!

Their devotion had pure, profound dimensions. For certain these women had other virtues, but they were content to give and give and give. Serving Jesus was the fulfillment of their lives. It was their purpose. Their sacrifice was merely a token of their gratitude.

Perhaps heightened by the countercultural esteem given them by Jesus, these women took Jesus seriously, maybe even more so than the men. Call it intuition or personal experience, but these women knew He was Messiah. After all, Jesus had rescued them: some from demonic terror, others from physical illness, all from spiritual darkness.

So they followed with tenacity and devotion, whatever the cost. They never boasted at how valuable they were to the company of followers, yet they were present in the two places and times when it mattered most—at the cross and the garden tomb.

They must have meant a great deal to Jesus who so notoriously and so openly broke culture's rules to help them—and He must have meant all the world to them. BP

Being used of God—is there anything more encouraging, more fulfilling? Perhaps not, but there is something more basic: meeting with God. Lingering in His presence, shutting out the noise of the city and, in quietness, giving Him the praise He deserves. Before we engage ourselves in His work, let's meet Him in His Word . . . in prayer . . . in worship.

—Chuck Swindoll

Giving OURSELVES

It's pretty easy for a woman to be persuaded that her value is directly related to her skill or appearance, her resume or status in the community. Current culture promotes that distortion.

But God's servants will surprise you. They know their true value lies in Christ. That awareness fills them up, and they overflow with love to others. They just simply see a need and try to meet it. They are eager to be of service in every way they can. Their goal is not to be great but to act on the great opportunity of serving the One who has saved them.

Take a step back and look at the women who serve the body of Christ at large. They are truly beautiful. Gracious hands doing hard labor. Wise eyes watching. Trustworthy ears listening. Discerning hearts shepherding. More than half the church today is comprised of strong-hearted women.

Women who encourage, counsel, and train. Others who assist in technical areas. Still more who organize and count. Dear ones who work with their hands, create, keep records, and run conferences. And all of them helping financially support the whole so it might operate smoothly and without a hitch. The body of Christ is truly in it *together*.

A servant does things you couldn't pay her to do. She knows she is owned by God and, therefore, is at God's disposal. That knowledge gives her freedom to serve without recognition or reward. But God does not forget. He sees every act of kindness, every gracious deed, and every sacrifice of time or focus. He is aware of every bit of energy spent. And He recognizes the love such women show as they serve the saints in His name.

Out of gratitude for all Jesus has done, from these women flow acts of generosity, courtesy, thoughtfulness, and sacrifice. Few qualities are more meaningful and impressive than a generous heart. Yes, that includes financial support, but perhaps more important than giving our money is giving ourselves. BP

What Every Woman Should KNOW

What you can and can't accomplish in a day, a month, and a year

That you can't change the length of your calves, the width of your hips, or the nature of your family

That Jesus loves you no matter what

That your childhood may not have been perfect but it's over and you survived

What you shouldn't take personally

When to say "when"

That men are not the "enemy"

That gentleness and kindness nurture real femininity

The fact that women were funding Jesus's ministry signaled a change in the greater New Testament culture. In prior generations, women were wholly financially dependent upon the male leadership in their families, unable to earn a sufficient living independently, own property, or receive an inheritance. Women having funds at their discretion indicated that the economic times were changing.

God Widens Our World

Shalini Patras

As director of International Development at Insight for Living, Shalini is continually amazed that God picked *her*, someone from a small, unknown town in India, and that He gives her an opportunity every day to serve Him in a ministry that impacts the world. At home, she focuses on loving and serving her daughter, Cela, and her partner in life and ministry, Vinay.

Lifetime Preparation for Ministry

"When I was a young girl, my family moved from Tuticorin to New Delhi—a world apart, even in our own country. The move taught me how to relate to people cross-culturally and helped me appreciate all kinds of climate and clothing, languages and cultures, senses of humor and even tastes."

What Translates the Same in Every Language?

"Love generously.
Give to everyone who asks of you.
Grow in character."

How Do You Believe God Uniquely Equips Women?

"Because we are women of God, we have large hearts to love our families, our friends, and yes, even those who irk us (as Jesus commands us to in Luke 6:27)."

What's One Lesson You've Learned from Your Mother?

"Never shy away from something difficult. Love all people well—rich, poor, sick, healthy."

God Is . . .

" . . . far more generous and far more loving than all of humankind put together!"

One of Shalini's Favorite Verses

This is love, not that we loved God, but that He loved us and sent His Son to be the propitiation for our sins. —1 John 4:10

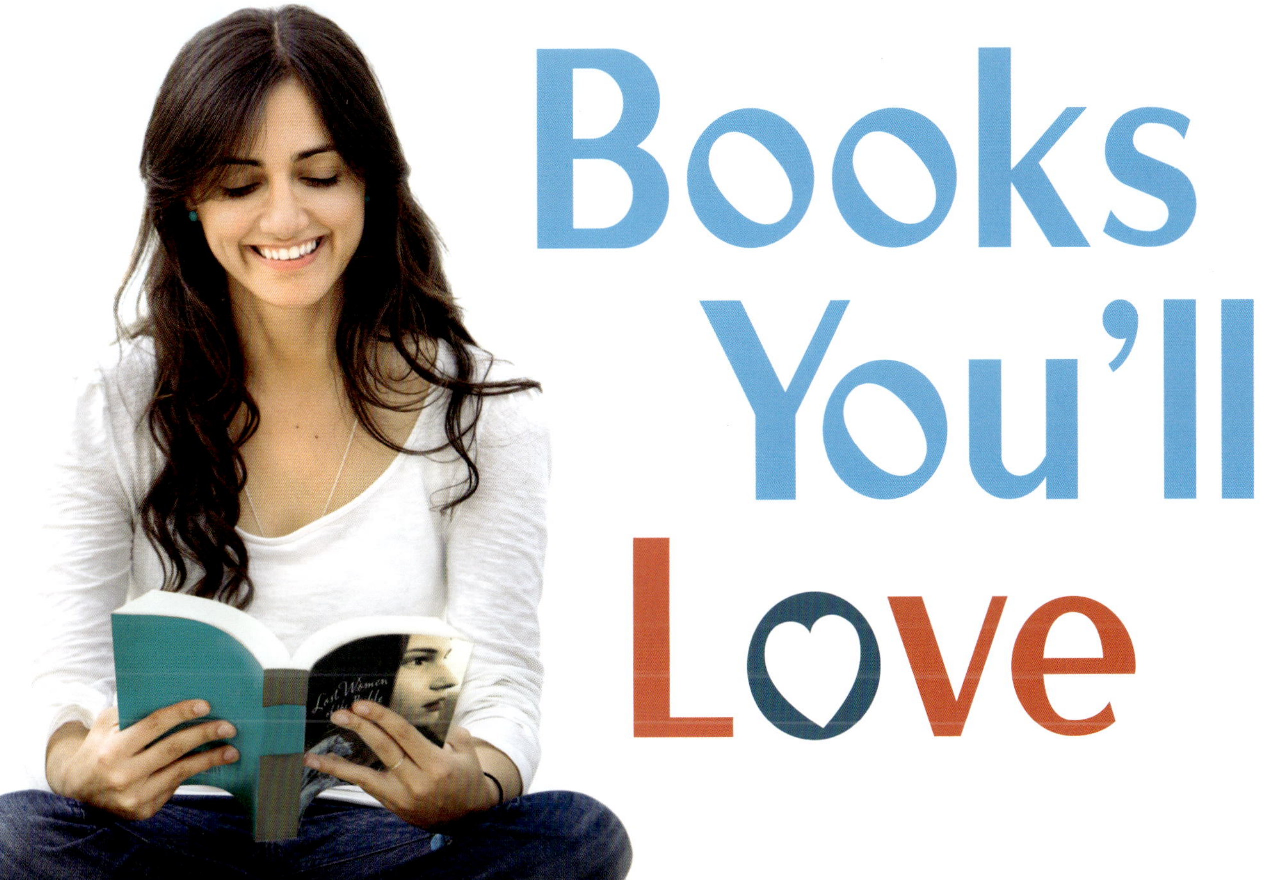

Books You'll Love

A Few of Our Favorite Books That We Think You'll Adore

Faith Is Not a Feeling: Choosing to Take God at His Word

by Ney Bailey

Meet Ney Bailey (see page 42). A wonderful, wise friend of Insight for Living, Ney wrote this classic book in response to a tragedy that rocked the Christian community—a flood that took the lives of one hundred fifty people, many of whom were her friends and coworkers. Deeply grieved by the loss, survivor Ney traveled a journey of faith to arrive at this conclusion: no matter how things look and no matter how we feel, God is in control.

Ney writes, "As you read this book, I pray that you will be encouraged and challenged, that God will strike fire in your heart, and that your life will be changed because you can say, 'Now I understand what it means to walk by faith. I understand that faith is not a feeling but a choice to take God at His word.'"

Faith Is Not a Feeling: Choosing to Take God at His Word by Ney Bailey. Colorado Springs: Waterbrook, 2002. 192-page softcover book.

Lost Women of the Bible: Finding Strength and Significance through Their Stories

by Carolyn Custis James

The ground has shifted under women today. We are not living in the world of our mothers and grandmothers. And our daughters' world will be different still. It's easy to feel lost between the opportunities and demands of the present and the biblical teaching of the past. Dallas Theological Seminary graduate Carolyn Custis James asks, "How do we reconcile the realities of contemporary culture with a more traditional idea of women's roles that seem out of step with the way we live today?"

The Bible offers a large vision of God's purpose for women—a vision that both encompasses the vast diversity of our lives and calls us to be more. Carolyn writes that these stories of the women of the Bible gave her "the freedom to embrace the life God was opening up for me." In this smart and engaging study, uncover insights into the biblical stories of women such as Eve, Hagar, Tamar, Hannah, and more that have been lost, muted, or passed over. *Lost Women of the Bible* brings the women of the Bible into the twenty-first century and recovers the power and relevance of their timeless message.

Lost Women of the Bible: Finding Strength and Significance through Their Stories by Carolyn Custis James. Grand Rapids: Zondervan, 2005. 240-page softcover book.

Esther: A Woman of Strength and Dignity

by Charles R. Swindoll

No one is born courageous. Courage grows out of difficult circumstances. Esther's story is an account of a woman thrust into a threatening situation that had no visible escape route.

Chuck Swindoll wrote,

> A mixture of uncertainty and danger lurks in the shadows as [Esther] finds herself virtually trapped in a no-win maze of circumstantial misery. . . .
>
> Unwittingly victimized by an unbearable situation, she stepped up . . . to make a difference. Throwing protocol to the wind and ignoring all her fears, this woman stood in a gap most of her peers would never have risked. In doing so, she . . . exposed and foiled the plans of an evil man [with] a violent agenda. She alone saved her nation from extermination. Now, that's what I call *power*!
>
> It's that kind of stuff that [made] writing this book such a delight.

Esther: A Woman of Strength and Dignity by Charles R. Swindoll. Nashville: Thomas Nelson, 1997. 224-page softcover book.

I Married Adventure: Looking at Life through the Lens of Possibility by Luci Swindoll. Nashville: Thomas Nelson, 2002. 210-page hardcover book.

I Married Adventure: Looking at Life through the Lens of Possibility

by Luci Swindoll

Ready or not—life is an adventure.

The concept of adventure may be scary to you—you may think it means traveling to remote places, wrestling wild animals, or jumping out of an airplane. "Not at all!" says Luci Swindoll. Adventure is "an attitude, not a behavior." It's looking at life through the lens of possibility. . . . It's "all about staying on the lookout—keeping our eyes and our hearts open and participating fully in the moment we've been given as a pure gift."

With all the winsomeness and wisdom you'd expect, Luci encourages you to transform otherwise regular days into experiences worth living.

- Stop saying, "if only" and "why me?" and start asking, "what if?" and "why not?"
- Capture each moment and savor the present—good or bad.
- Let go of your regrets and embrace your dreams.

Dare to dream big, gain a new perspective on life, take risks and, above all, embrace life as a wonderful adventure.

The Wise and the Wild: 30 Devotions on Women of the Bible

by Charles R. Swindoll and Insight for Living

You've at least casually met these thirty women if you've been around the Bible for any time. Their names and stories ring a bell. Some are wise, others wild—all of them at crossroads of choice, confronting their culture and times. Now you can spend a few minutes one-on-one with these women that God chose to highlight in His Word. Get a realistic look at them and perhaps you'll catch a glimpse of your own story in theirs. Chuck Swindoll and the staff of Insight for Living offer down-to-earth portraits of thirty godly—and not so godly—women so that you can learn from their examples how to make wise choices and answer the call to a deeper faith in God.

Available exclusively from Insight for Living.

The Wise and the Wild: 30 Devotions on Women of the Bible by Charles R. Swindoll and Insight for Living. Plano, Tex.: IFL Publishing House, 2010. 135-page spiral bound softcover book.

How to Begin a Relationship with God

The life and ministry of Jesus Christ was a revolution in human history. No person has caused more of a stir, broken more conventions, or challenged more traditions of human invention than Jesus. He was controversial. For example, the world of Jesus's day said that a woman's testimony in court was suspect unless confirmed by witnesses. And yet it was a woman to whom Jesus gave the honor of being the first to testify about His resurrection. Her testimony was controversial . . . but it was life-changing to all who would listen. It pointed to the truth of how men and women alike can have a relationship with God by having a relationship with Jesus Christ.

If you'd like to find out how you can have a relationship with God, the Bible marks the path with four essential truths. Let's look at each marker in detail.

Our Spiritual Condition: *Totally Depraved*

The first truth is rather personal. One look in the mirror of Scripture, and our human condition becomes painfully clear:

> "There is none righteous, not even one;
> There is none who understands,
> There is none who seeks for God;
> All have turned aside, together they
> have become useless;
> There is none who does good,
> There is not even one."
> (Romans 3:10–12)

We are all sinners through and through—totally depraved. Now, that doesn't mean we've committed every atrocity known to humankind. We're not as *bad* as we can be, just as *bad off* as we can be. Sin colors all our thoughts, motives, words, and actions.

If you've been around a while, you likely already believe it. Look around. Everything around us bears the smudge marks of our sinful nature. Despite our best efforts to create a perfect world, crime statistics continue to soar, divorce rates keep climbing, and families keep crumbling.

Something has gone terribly wrong in our society and in ourselves—something deadly. Contrary to how the world would repackage it, "me-first" living doesn't equal rugged individuality and freedom; it equals death. As Paul said in his letter to the Romans, "The wages of sin is death" (Romans 6:23)—our spiritual and physical death that comes from God's righteous judgment of our sin, along with all of the emotional and practical effects of this separation that we experience on a daily basis. This brings us to the second marker: God's character.

God's Character: *Infinitely Holy*

How can God judge us for a sinful state we were born into? Our total depravity is only half the answer. The other half is God's infinite holiness.

The fact that we know things are not as they should be points us to a standard of goodness beyond ourselves. Our sense of injustice in life on this side of eternity implies a perfect standard of justice beyond our reality. That standard and source is God Himself. And God's standard of holiness contrasts starkly with our sinful condition.

Scripture says that "God is Light, and in Him there is no darkness at all" (1 John 1:5). God is absolutely holy—which creates a problem for us. If He is so pure, how can we who are so impure relate to Him?

Perhaps we could try being better people, try to tilt the balance in favor of our good deeds, or seek out methods for self-improvement. Throughout history, people have attempted to live up to God's standard by keeping the Ten Commandments or living by their own code of ethics. Unfortunately, no one can come close to satisfying the demands of God's law. Romans 3:20 says, "By the works of the Law no flesh will be justified in His sight; for through the Law comes the knowledge of sin."

Our Need: *A Substitute*

So here we are, sinners by nature and sinners by choice, trying to pull ourselves up by our own bootstraps to attain a relationship with our holy Creator. But every time we try, we fall flat on our faces. We can't live a good enough life to make up for our sin, because God's standard isn't "good enough"—it's *perfection*. And we can't make amends for the offense our sin has created without dying for it.

Who can get us out of this mess?

If someone could live perfectly, honoring God's law, and would bear sin's death penalty for us—in our place—then we would be saved from our predicament. But is there such a person? Thankfully, yes!

Meet your substitute—*Jesus Christ*. He is the One who took death's place for you!

> [God] made [Jesus Christ] who knew no sin to be sin on our behalf, so that we might become the righteousness of God in Him. (2 Corinthians 5:21)

God's Provision: *A Savior*

God rescued us by sending His Son, Jesus, to die on the cross for our sins (1 John 4:9–10). Jesus was fully human and fully divine (John 1:1, 18), a truth that ensures His understanding of our weaknesses, His power to forgive, and His ability to bridge the gap between God and us (Romans 5:6–11). In short, we are "justified as a gift by His grace through the redemption which is in Christ Jesus" (Romans 3:24). Two words in this verse bear further explanation: *justified* and *redemption*.

Justification is God's act of mercy, in which He declares righteous the believing sinners while we are still in our sinning state. Justification doesn't mean that God *makes* us righteous, so that we never sin again, rather that He *declares* us righteous—much like a judge pardons a guilty criminal. Because Jesus took our sin upon Himself and suffered our judgment on the cross, God forgives our debt and proclaims us PARDONED.

Redemption is Christ's act of paying the complete price to release us from sin's bondage. God sent His Son to bear His wrath for all of our sins—past, present, and future (Romans 3:24–26; 2 Corinthians 5:21). In humble obedience, Christ willingly endured the shame of the cross for our sake (Mark 10:45; Romans 5:6–8; Philippians 2:8). Christ's death satisfied God's righteous demands. He no longer holds our sins against us, because His own Son paid the penalty for them. We are freed from the slave market of sin, never to be enslaved again!

Placing Your Faith in Christ

These four truths describe how God has provided a way to Himself through Jesus Christ. Because the price has been paid in full by God, we must respond to His free gift of eternal life in total faith and confidence in Him to save us. We must step forward into the relationship with God that He has prepared for us—not by doing good works or by being a good person, but by coming to Him just as we are and accepting His justification and redemption by faith.

> For by grace you have been saved through faith; and that not of yourselves, it is the gift of God; not as a result of works, so that no one may boast. (Ephesians 2:8–9)

We accept God's gift of salvation simply by placing our faith in Christ alone for the forgiveness of our sins. Would you like to enter a relationship with your Creator by trusting in Christ as your Savior? If so, here's a simple prayer you can use to express your faith:

Dear God,

I know that my sin has put a barrier between You and me. Thank You for sending Your Son, Jesus, to die in my place. I trust in Jesus alone to forgive my sins, and I accept His gift of eternal life. I ask Jesus to be my personal Savior and the Lord of my life. Thank You. In Jesus's name, amen.

If you've prayed this prayer or one like it and you wish to find out more about knowing God and His plan for you in the Bible, contact us at Insight for Living. Our contact information is on the following page.

We Are Here for YOU

If you desire to find out more about knowing God and His plan for you in the Bible, contact us. Insight for Living provides staff pastors who are available for free written correspondence or phone consultation. These seminary-trained and seasoned counselors have years of experience and are well-qualified guides for your spiritual journey.

Please feel welcome to contact your regional Pastoral Ministries by using the following information:

United States
Insight for Living
Pastoral Ministries
Post Office Box 269000
Plano, Texas 75026-9000
USA
972-473-5097, Monday through Friday, 8:00 a.m.–5:00 p.m. central time
www.insight.org/contactapastor

Canada
Insight for Living Canada
Pastoral Ministries
PO Box 8 Stn A
Abbotsford BC V2T 6Z4
CANADA
1-800-663-7639
info@insightforliving.ca

Australia, New Zealand, and South Pacific
Insight for Living Australia
Pastoral Care
Post Office Box 443
Boronia, VIC 3155
AUSTRALIA
1300 467 444

United Kingdom and Europe
Insight for Living United Kingdom
Pastoral Care
PO Box 553
Dorking
RH4 9EU
UNITED KINGDOM
0800 915 9364
+44 (0)1306 640156
pastoralcare@insightforliving.org.uk

ENDNOTES

1. Betty Scott Stam, quoted in Kathleen White, *John and Betty Stam* (Minneapolis: Bethany House, 1989), 118.
2. Martin Luther, *Defense and Explanation of All the Articles*, quoted in Warren Wiersbe, *The Wiersbe Bible Commentary: The Complete Old Testament in One Volume* (Colorado Springs: David C. Cook, 2007), 145.
3. Adapted from Charles R. Swindoll, *Swindoll's New Testament Insights: Insights on John* (Grand Rapids: Zondervan, 2010), 163–64.
4. Adapted from Swindoll, *Insights on John*, 163–64.
5. Adapted from Charles R. Swindoll, *Embraced by the Spirit: The Untold Blessings of Intimacy with God* (Grand Rapids: Zondervan, 2010), 89–90, 116–17.
6. Robert Lowry, "Nothing but the Blood," in *The Celebration Hymnal: Songs and Hymns for Worship* (Nashville: Word/ Integrity, 1997), hymn 337.
7. Francois Fenelon, as quoted in Charles R. Swindoll, *Strengthening Your Grip: Essentials in an Aimless World* (Dallas: Word, 1982), 157–58.
8. W. Hall Harris, ed., *The NET Bible Notes*, 1st Accordance electronic ed. (Richardson, Tex.: Biblical Studies Press, 2005), n.p.
9. Adam Clarke, *Adam Clarke's Commentary on the Whole Bible*, Accordance electronic ed. 6 vols. (Altamonte Springs, Fla.: OakTree Software, 2004), n.p.
10. Charles R. Swindoll, *The Quest for Character: Inspirational Thoughts for Becoming More Like Christ* (Grand Rapids: Zondervan, 1982), 115–16.
11. Adapted from Charles R. Swindoll, *Improving Your Serve*, (Nashville: Thomas Nelson, 1981), 19–21.
12. D. A. Carson, *Matthew*, in EBC 8; ed. Frank E. Gaebelein and J. D. Douglas, Accordance electronic ed. (Grand Rapids: Zondervan, 1984), n.p.; Tacitus, *The Annals*, 3.33–35, accessed January 20, 2011 from http://mcadams.posc.mu.edu/txt/ah/tacitus/ TacitusAnnals03.html).
13. Robert H. Mounce, *Matthew*, in *NIBC* 1, Accordance electronic ed. 18 vols. (Peabody, Mass.: Hendrickson, 1991), 254–55.
14. Adapted from Charles R. Swindoll, "Think with Discernment," in *Make Up Your Mind . . . About the Issues of Life* (Portland, Ore.: Multnomah, 1981), 12–13.
15. Persian proverb, as quoted in Charles R. Swindoll, *Make Up Your Mind . . . About the Issues of Life* (Portland, Ore.: Multnomah, 1981), 12.
16. Flavius Josephus and William Whitson, *The Works of Josephus: Complete and Unabridged*, Wars 5.176 (1987; Peabody, Mass.: Hendrickson, 1996).
17. Adapted from Wayne Stiles, *Walking in the Footsteps of Jesus: A Journey Through the Lands and Lessons of Christ* (Ventura, Calif.: Regal, 2008), 150–51. Used by permission.

About the Writers

Charles R. Swindoll

Charles R. Swindoll has devoted his life to the clear, practical teaching and application of God's Word and His grace. A pastor at heart, Chuck has served as senior pastor to congregations in Texas, Massachusetts, and California. He currently pastors Stonebriar Community Church in Frisco, Texas, but Chuck's listening audience extends far beyond a local church body. As a leading program in Christian broadcasting, *Insight for Living* airs in major Christian radio markets around the world, reaching people groups in languages they can understand. Chuck's extensive writing ministry has also served the body of Christ worldwide and his leadership as president and now chancellor of Dallas Theological Seminary has helped prepare and equip a new generation for ministry. Chuck and Cynthia, his partner in life and ministry, have four grown children and ten grandchildren.

(DJ) *Derrick G. Jeter*

Strong-willed and wise women have always been a part of Derrick's life. Growing up as the only boy among two sisters and living near two grandmothers with forceful personalities, Derrick learned early on to respect the wisdom of women. Now, after more than twenty years of marriage to Christy and five children, one of whom is a teenage daughter, he has learned to admire a woman's wisdom. Derrick is a graduate of Dallas Theological Seminary and serves as a writer for Insight for Living.

(BP) *Barb Peil*

As one of the first women to graduate from Dallas Theological Seminary, Barb knows what it's like to be a woman in a man's world. But it doesn't scare her. Far from it, she counts herself especially blessed to have enjoyed a couple of decades (so far) in ministry in the world of education, writing, and Christian radio. Barb received her master of arts in Christian Education from Dallas Theological Seminary and serves as managing editor and assistant writer at Insight for Living.

(WS) *Wayne Stiles*

After serving in the pastorate for fourteen years, Wayne Stiles joined the staff at Insight for Living and currently serves as executive vice president and chief content officer. He received his master of theology and doctor of ministry degrees from Dallas Theological Seminary. Wayne and his wife, Cathy, have two teenage daughters.

Ordering Information

If you would like to order additional copies of Women in the Life of Jesus or order other Insight for Living resources, please contact the office that serves you.

United States
Insight for Living
Post Office Box 269000
Plano, Texas 75026-9000
USA
1-800-772-8888
(Monday through Friday,
7:00 a.m. – 7:00 p.m. Central time)
www.insight.org

Canada
Insight for Living Canada
PO Box 8 Stn A
Abbotsford BC V2T 6Z4
CANADA
1-800-663-7639
www.insightforliving.ca

Australia, New Zealand, and South Pacific
Insight for Living Australia
Post Office Box 443
Boronia, VIC 3155
AUSTRALIA
1300 467 444
www.insight.asn.au

United Kingdom and Europe
Insight for Living United Kingdom
PO Box 553
Dorking
RH4 9EU
UNITED KINGDOM
0800 915 9364
www.insightforliving.org.uk

Other International Locations
International constituents may contact the U.S. office through our Web site (www.insightworld.org), mail queries, or by calling +1-972-473-5136.